# THE FRAUDSTER

# (LE FAISEUR, OU MERCADET)

A Comedy in Five Acts

*Honoré de Balzac*
*Translated by*
*Laurence Senelick*

BROADWAY PLAY PUBLISHING INC
New York
www.broadwayplaypublishing.com
info@broadwayplaypublishing.com

THE FRAUDSTER


Cover art *Macaire as Speculator* by Honoré Daumier

First edition: September 2022
I S B N: 978-0-88145-937-1

Book design: Marie Donovan
Page make-up: Adobe InDesign
Typeface: Palatino

# TRANSLATOR'S NOTE

Like many great novelists—Dickens, Dostoevsky, Henry James—Balzac wanted to make a name as a successful playwright. In his particular case, he hoped it would earn him the money to pay off his cumbersome debts. He failed to achieve this in his lifetime, not for want of talent at dialogue and intrigue, but because his dynamic ideas and pungent language rarely fit the well-carpentered box that was the stage of his time.

There is no lack of variety in his plays: LA MARÂTRE (THE STEP-MOTHER) is a domestic drama that moves the incestuous theme of Phaedra to a middle-class drawing-room and inspired Turgenev's A MONTH IN THE COUNTRY. VAUTRIN concerns a master criminal whose underworld machinations provoke scandals in the highest society. LES RESSOURCES DE QUINOLA (QUINOLA'S STRATEGIES) is a tragicomedy set in the Spain of the Inquisition.

The best of the lot is LE FAISEUR, OU MERCADET (THE FRAUDSTER) No French-English dictionary provides an adequate translation of the title. A *faiseur* can, however, be perfectly translated into Yiddish—a *makher*, someone who lives by doing deals, who has a finger in every pie. These deals may not be technically legal or scrupulous, but a *faiseur* is not a swindler or a conman in any legal sense. Mercadet and his associates always operate on the very brink of lawlessness but never go over it.

As a word, *le faiseur* was newly coined, because it described a recent phenomenon: a burgeoning middle class whose prosperity came from the circulation of money. Money always makes Balzac's world go round and in this comedy, the Stock Exchange is Mercadet's playground. In the first hundred lines, money or its surrogates (francs, cents, taxes, lease, debtor, creditor, pay, bankruptcy, etc) are mentioned sixty-eight times. Stocks and shares, loans and promissory notes are the motors of the plot. Derring-do and noble sentiments are replaced by underhanded deals and backstairs negotiations. Talk of love plays second fiddle to discussions of dowries and settlements. (Mercadet's daughter Julie is something new in drama: a homely girl of sense and sensibility; her beloved is an equally complicated figure.)

Compare the dynamic use of money to such earlier plays as Molière's MISER. Harpagon may be in love with his cashbox, but the coins in it lie inert and unexploited. Jonson's Volpone uses the lure of money to increase his wealth, but this remains a private enterprise and the gold sleeps in a chest by his bed. Mercadet is no miser; he is a dreamer, a sleepwalker on a rooftop, apt to fall at any moment. He juggles millions and promotes projects, both real and imaginary. Money is not an end or a passion, but his element, his nervous system, the underlying principle of his life.

Mercadet thinks and acts on a heroic scale, regularly comparing himself to Napoleon. The Empire was a distant memory when Balzac wrote LE FAISEUR over the course of ten years, finishing it in 1839. During that decade there was an epidemic of creating banks and joint-stock companies. France at the time was ruled by Louis-Philippe, the "Citizen King," who carried an umbrella and led a blameless personal life. The motto of his reign was François Guizot's "Enrichissez-vous par le travail et l'épargne!" ("Get rich by work and savings!") Steam engines and coal were the motors of industry, but power was held by an oligarchy of financiers and businessmen, the "ventrigoulus" or "greedy-guts" seen in Daumier's caricatures. They also teem with *chevaliers d'industrie*, sharpers and crooks on the lookout for the main chance.

Balzac's unblinking vision of this get-rich-quick society was probably too honest a mirror for the audiences of the time, which is why LE FAISEUR (under the title MERCADET) was not staged until 1851, a year after its author's death. By then, a spectacular bubble in railway stocks had burst, ruining many investors including Balzac. An impoverished population had fomented a social revolution in 1848, leading to the Second Republic. Getting and spending were no longer trumpeted as society's greatest aims.

When it finally reached the stage, Balzac's five-act comedy was reduced to three by the popular melodramatist Adolphe d'Ennery. He pruned the play of a few characters, the most theatrical moments (De la Brive's disguise, for instance) and some of Balzac's most pungent lines. Sentimentality was pumped up and cynicism played down. In the twentieth century, LE FAISEUR was periodically produced as a showcase for an outstanding character actor—Charles Dullin, Jean Vilar, Bernard Blier—, filmed and televised. In the age of Bernie Madoff and his epigones, it has been revived as a timely precursor, even in a modern-dress production set in the 1970s.

In all these cases, the script was "adapted," less radically perhaps than by d'Ennery, but still abridged or compacted, its incidents reshuffled. The current translation is based on the complete text revised by Balzac in 1848. It attempts to be as faithful as possible to that original, preserving the whole play. It is up to potential directors or dramaturges to make the cuts and transpositions they may find necessary. The play's "relevance" to current financial crises and scandals does not need a language conforming to the latest slang. It is self-evident.

For modern audiences, an intriguing aspect of LE FAISEUR is the regular mention of "waiting for Godeau," The putative return of Monsieur Godeau, Mercadet's former partner who absconded with a good deal of their working capital many years before and is reputed to be in the East Indies, is supposed to clear up their debts and justify new loans. He never appears on stage. In this post-Beckett world, the allusion seems more than coincidental, even though Samuel Beckett denied ever having heard of Balzac's play when he wrote EN ATTENDANT GODOT. Whatever the case, the coincidence lends an aura of existentialism to the otherwise highly material ambience of Mercadet's world.

**Laurence Senelick**, Medford, Mass., 2022

# CHARACTERS & SETTING

AUGUSTE MERCADET, *a speculator*
ALICE MERCADET, *his wife*
JULIE, *their daughter*
ADOLPHE MINARD, *a book-keeper*
BRÉDIF, MERCADET'*s landlord*
VERDELIN, MERCADET'*s friend*
GOULARD, *a businessman,* MERCADET'*s creditor*
PIERQUIN, *a money lender,* MERCADET'*s creditor*
VIOLETTE, *a money lender,* MERCADET'*s creditor*
BERCHUT, MERCADET'*s unlicensed broker*
MICHONNIN DE LA BRIVE, *an elegant young man*
DE MÉRICOURT, *another young man*
JUSTIN, *valet,* MERCADET'*s servant*
THÉRÈSE, *maid,* MERCADET'*s servant*
VIRGINIE, *cook,* MERCADET'*s servant*

*Scene: Paris, the main drawing-room in* MERCADET'*s apartment.*

*Time: 1839*

# ACT ONE

(BRÉDIF *is alone on stage.)*

BRÉDIF: An eleven-room apartment, top-notch, right in the heart of Paris! …And a mere two thousand five hundred francs! I lose three thousand francs by it every year…ever since the July Revolution. Ah! the most inconvenient thing about revolutions is that sudden decline in rents…I should never have drawn up a lease in 1830! …Luckily, Monsieur Mercadet owes a year and a half's back rent, there's a lien on his furniture, and, if I sell it…

MERCADET: *(Enters, having heard the last words)* Sell my furniture! And you got up at the crack of dawn to make your fellow-man miserable?

BRÉDIF: You're not my fellow-man, thank God, Monsieur Mercadet! …You're head over ears in debt, whereas I don't owe a penny. I am in a building I own and you are my tenant.

MERCADET: Ah, of course! Equality has never been more than a word! We shall always be split into two classes: debtors and creditors, as the English so neatly put it. Come, be French, my dear Monsieur Brédif, your hand!

BRÉDIF: I'd rather you hand over my rent, my dear Monsieur Mercadet.

MERCADET: You're the only one of my creditors who's got collateral from me—actual collateral! Eighteen months ago you put a lien on my furniture, inventoried piece by piece, with the greatest care, furniture worth fifteen thousand francs, and the two years' rent won't be owing for another... four months.

BRÉDIF: And the interest on my capital? ...I'm losing it.

MERCADET: Sue me! ...I'll plead guilty.

BRÉDIF: My dear monsieur Mercadet, I don't go in for speculation! I live on my income. If all my tenants were like you... No, we must put an end to this...

MERCADET: What, my dear Monsieur Brédif, I've lived in your building for eleven years and you're throwing me out? You who's privy to my ups and down, a witness to all my efforts! Surely you know I'm the victim of Godeau's abuse of my confidence...

BRÉDIF: Godeau? ...Are you going to sing me that old tune about your partner absconding—I know it by heart and so do all your creditors. After all, Monsieur Godeau...

MERCADET: Godeau? ...Whenever a writer describes a con-man, I assume he knew Godeau!...

BRÉDIF: Why bad-mouth Godeau! He was a fellow of rare energy, a man about town! ...Living with a little lady...very tasty...

MERCADET: By whom he had a child they abandoned...

BRÉDIF: Bah, Duval your ex-cashier, was moved by that charming lady's pleas and adopted the young man, didn't he?

MERCADET: And Godeau adopted our strong-box.

BRÉDIF: He borrowed from you a hundred and fifty thousand francs... by violence, I agree. But he left you all the other stocks and bonds in your firm's liquidation...and you went on doing business! For eight years you made enormous profits! You won...

MERCADET: Victories on paper! It's not uncommon among us speculators.

BRÉDIF: But didn't Monsieur Godeau promise to cut you in for half the profits of his ventures in India? He will return!

MERCADET: Is that so? Then you wait for Godeau! And that way you'll get the interest on your rent, won't that be an excellent investment?

BRÉDIF: That's an eloquent rationale; but if all landlords listened to their tenants, all the tenants would pay them in this coin, and the government...

MERCADET: What's the government got to do with it? or anyone.

BRÉDIF: The government wants its taxes and can't be paid with rationales. Therefore, I regret I am forced to take harsh measures!

MERCADET: And I thought you were such a nice fellow! Aren't you aware I'm about to marry off my daughter... Let me get past the wedding! You're invited... Come along! Madame Brédif will dance at it! ...I may pay you the day after.

BRÉDIF: The day after...it is the day after. I'm very sorry if I frighten away your son-in-law, but you should have received my little distraint day before yesterday, and if you don't pay today, the auction notices go up tomorrow.

MERCADET: Ah! this distraint freezes the claims of my other creditors and you want me to pay for that protection? Well, what can I offer to gain me three months?

BRÉDIF: A strict conscience might boggle to agree to such reluctant complicity, for it would mean hoodwinking…

MERCADET: Who?

BRÉDIF: Your son-in-law to-be…

MERCADET: *(Aside)* The old crook!…

BRÉDIF: But I'm a decent fellow. Give up the right to sub-let and I'll leave you in peace for three months.

MERCADET: Ah! A man in trouble is like a crumb thrown in a fish-tank! Every fish takes a bite. And my creditors are barracudas! …They won't stop until the debtor, like the crumb, is gobbled up. Let's see, is this 1839? My lease has seven years to run, then you're allowed to double the rent.

BRÉDIF: Fortunately for us!

MERCADET: Well! I know in three months you'll throw me out and my unhappy wife will have lost the resource of that sub-let she's counting on in case of…

BRÉDIF: Insolvency?

MERCADET: Oh, what a word! …Poison to an honest man! …Monsieur Brédif, can't you see what corrupts even the most honorable debtors? …I'll tell you: the crafty ploys of certain creditors who, to make a few pennies, stretch the law to the point of theft.

BRÉDIF: Sir, I came here to be paid, not to hear what's poison to an honest man.

MERCADET: Oh, debt! People regard debt as worse than crime… Crime puts a roof over your head, debt puts you out on the street. Well, I'm wrong, sir, I'm at your disposal, I will give up my right.

BRÉDIF: *(Aside)* If he had done so graciously, I would have been indulgent. But to tell me I'm selling him out... *(Aloud)* Sir, I don't want your grudging consent...I'm not a man to put people on the rack.

MERCADET: You want me to thank you!... *(Aside)* Temper, temper. *(Aloud)* I may have been too hasty, my dear Monsieur Brédif, but I'm being cruelly persecuted! ...Not one of my creditors realizes I'm fighting to make sure I can pay them.

BRÉDIF: You mean, make sure you can go on doing business.

MERCADET: Of course, sir! Where would I be if I didn't preserve the right to trade on the Stock Exchange?

*(*JUSTIN *appears in the doorway.)*

BRÉDIF: Then let's conclude this little transaction...

MERCADET: Please, not in front of the servants. I have a hard enough time now keeping them in line. Let's go down to your place.

BRÉDIF: *(Aside)* I'll have my apartment back in three months.

*(*MERCADET *and* BRÉDIF *exit.)*

JUSTIN: Poor Monsieur Mercadet, it's sink or swim and he can't keep his head above water! Although you can still turn a profit from employers who are hard-up, he owes me a year's wages, so it's time to get fired. The landlord looks likely to kick us out. Nowadays the master's disrepute brings the servants down too. Tradesmen are forcing me to pay for what I buy... It's a nuisance.

*(*THÉRÈSE *and* VIRGINIE *enter.)*

THÉRÈSE: Do you think this'll go on much longer, Monsieur Justin?

VIRGINIE: I've worked in lots of middle-class households, but I've never seen anything like this!

I'm going to give up cooking and be an actress on the stage.

JUSTIN: We're all nothing but actors on a stage!

VIRGINIE: Sometimes you have to look surprised, like you've dropped from the moon, when a creditor shows up: "Didn't you know, sir?"—"No."—"Monsieur Mercadet has gone to Lyons."—"He's away?" "Yes, on a wonderful piece of business! He's discovered coal mines."—"Ah! Good for him! When does he get back?"—"We don't know." Sometimes I make a face like I've just lost the thing I hold most dear in the world.

JUSTIN: *(Aside)* Her money.

VIRGINIE: "Monsieur and his daughter are in the greatest distress. Madame Mercadet, poor lady! It seems we're about to lose her—They've taken her away for the salt-water cure."—"Ah!"

THÉRÈSE: With me it's always the same routine. "You want Monsieur Mercadet?"—"Yes, mam'selle."—"He's not in."—"He's not in?"—"No, but if the gentleman has come to see his daughter... she's all by herself!" And they turn tail and run for their lives! Poor Mam'selle Julie, if she was beautiful, they'd make her into...something.

JUSTIN: Some of these creditors are as rude as if you were the masters.

VIRGINIE: But what's the point of being a creditor? So far as I can see, they waste their time coming and going, spying on the master and spending whole hours listening to his talk.

JUSTIN: It's a great profession! They're all rich.

THÉRÈSE: But they've all given their money to the master and he doesn't give it back.

VIRGINIE: That's what I call stealing!

JUSTIN: Borrowing isn't stealing. Virginie, that word is not admitted in the Board of Trade. Listen! I take money out of your bag unbeknownst to you, you've been robbed. But if I say "Virginie, I need a hundred sous, lend them to me?" You hand them over, I don't give them back, I'm hard up, I'll reimburse you later, then you become my creditor! Do you understand, country girl?

VIRGINIE: No! If I don't get my money one way or another, what difference does it make! Ah! my wages are overdue, I'll ask for what's owed me and turn in my grocery accounts. The thing is, the shopkeepers refuse to sell anything except for cash. I'm not going to put out any of mine.

THÉRÈSE: I've already been impertinent to the mistress a couple of times, and she pretends to ignore me!…

JUSTIN: . Let's demand our wages!..

VIRGINIE: Are they really middle class? —Middle-class people spend a lot on their groceries—

JUSTIN: Are devoted to their servants—

VIRGINIE: And leave them an annuity for life! That's how middle-class people are supposed to behave to their servants.

THÉRÈSE: Well said, country girl! Well, I don't intend to leave. I want to know how it all comes out, it's fun to watch! I read Mam'selle's letters, I torment her boyfriend, that little Minard who she'll probably marry. She must have said something about it to her father. They've ordered dresses, bonnets, hats, in short whole outfits for the mistress and her daughter. Then, yesterday, the tradesmen refused to deliver.

VIRGINIE: If there's a wedding, we'll all get tips. We should stay till the day after the wedding.

JUSTIN: You think Monsieur Mercadet is going to marry his daughter to a little book-keeper who earns no more than eighteen hundred francs? *(He reads the newspapers.)*

THÉRÈSE: I'm sure of it! They adore one another. The mistress, who goes out every night and leaves her daughter at home, hasn't a clue about the affair. Little Minard comes as soon as Mam'selle is alone, and since they haven't taken me into their confidence, I go in, make a fuss, eavesdrop on them. Oh! they're very well behaved. Mam'selle, like all homely young ladies, wants to be sure she's loved for herself. She works at her china painting, while the fellow pretends to read novels to her, it's been like that for three months now... Mam'selle gets around it by saying to her mother later that night, "Mama, Monsieur Minard came to see you, so I received him."

VIRGINIE: You listen in on them?

THÉRÈSE: Why not? Mam'selle acts like she's afraid of being interrupted, so she leaves the doors open.

VIRGINIE: I'd love to know what bosses say when they're courting.

THÉRÈSE: Silly things! They talk about deals!...

JUSTIN: You mean, ideals.

THÉRÈSE: Look, I've copied out one of his letters to see if I could use it.

JUSTIN: Read it to us...

THÉRÈSE: 'My angel."

VIRGINIE: Oh, my angel!

THÉRÈSE: It's so sweet when someone takes you round the waist and whispers "my angel." "My angel, yes, I do love you; but do you love a poor disinherited fellow like myself? You would love me if you only knew how much love there is in the soul of a heretofore spurned young man, when love is all he has. Yesterday I read radiant hopes in your face. I believed in a happy future. You converted my doubts into certainty, my weakness into strength. At last your glances cured me of the malady of doubt…"

VIRGINIE: It curdles my brain! …You can't make head or tail of such talk! …Is that love lingo? …Love should go right to the point! Here, tell me what you think of a letter I got from a cute young fellow, a student in the Latin Quarter… No riddles about it, it's clear as day, and won't make your head ache. I know it by heart. "Charming female! (That's as good as my angel!) charming female! Meet me, I insist. In a case like this, people claim they have a thousand things to say. I have only one I'll repeat a hundred times if you don't stop me the first time." And it's signed Hypolite.

JUSTIN: Well, what did he say? Did you stick with him?

VIRGINIE: I never saw him again. He ran into me at the Chaumière café, he must have known who I was, and the idiot blushed when he saw I was wearing an apron.

JUSTIN: Oh, well! Now listen to what old Grumeau the concierge just told me! …Yesterday, while we were out running errands, two handsome young men drove up in an open carriage. Their groom told him that one of the gents was going to marry Mam'selle Mercadet. Then that gent gave old Grumeau a hundred francs.

VIRGINIE & THÉRÈSE: *(Astonished)* A hundred francs!..

JUSTIN: Yes, a hundred francs, not a promise, and in silver! Old Grumeau had learned his lesson so well, he pretended to let the groom pump him and told him our master's so rich he doesn't know how much money he has…

VIRGINIE: Those must be the two young men in yellow gloves and beautiful embroidered silk waistcoats. Their carriage gleamed like satin, their horses had roses here *(she points to her ears)* It was held by a boy of eight, with curly blond hair, top boots, the look of a mouse nibbling lace, a Cupid with dazzling linen who swore like a trooper. And that handsome young man who owns it, with big diamonds in his cravat, is to marry Mam'selle Mercadet! ...Don't make me laugh!

THÉRÈSE: Mam'selle?...with the face of an heiress with nothing to inherit? Don't make me laugh!

VIRGINIE: Ah, she does sing nicely! I hear her sometimes and it's lovely. I'd like to know how to sing like her: "A fortune sweet is at my feet."

JUSTIN: You don't know Monsieur Mercadet! ...I've been with him for six years, and ever since he took a tumble sparring with his creditors, I believe him capable of anything, even getting rich again... Sometimes I think he's totally ruined! Yellow auction posters bloom on his door, there are reams of official summonses I sell as waste paper behind his back! But presto! Up he bobs, triumphant! And so inventive! ... You don't read the papers, you lot! There's something new every day: wooden sidewalks, sidewalks spun from gold; investments in dukedoms, mills, even laundries... It's a shame! ...I really don't know why there's a hole in his safe! He fills it up and it empties out like a wine-glass! ...One day the master goes to bed a dead beat, the next day he wakes up a millionaire because he works awfully hard. He figures, he calculates, he writes prospectuses that act like wolf traps and always catch investors. But for all the projects he launches, he always has creditors. He sends them packing, he has them going in circles! Ah! sometimes they show up planning to make off with everything and throw him in prison! He talks to them… Well! they end up laughing together and leave the best friends in the world. Creditors begin by screeching like peacocks, cursing like stevedores, and end with "My dear Mercadet" and shaking hands all round. You see, when a man can talk down people like that Pierquin…

THÉRÈSE: A tiger who feeds on thousand-franc bank notes…

JUSTIN: Or poor old Violette!

VIRGINIE: Ah! poor dear fellow, I always feel inclined to give him table scraps…

JUSTIN: Or Goulard!

THÉRÈSE: Goulard! A loan shark who'd like to sink his teeth… into me!

JUSTIN: He's rich, he's a bachelor! Let him…

VIRGINIE: I hear the mistress coming.

JUSTIN: Let's be discreet and we're bound to learn more about this marriage…

*(Enter* MME MERCADET.*)*

MME MERCADET: Have you seen the master?

THÉRÈSE: Madam got up by herself without ringing for me!

MME MERCADET: Monsieur Mercadet is not in his room, I was worried, so…Justin, do you know where the master is?

JUSTIN: The master was arguing with Monsieur Brédif and they are….

MME MERCADET: All right… That'll do, Justin…

JUSTIN: The master has not left the building.

MME MERCADET: Thank you!

THÉRÈSE: Madam must be cross that they refused to deliver the things you ordered...

VIRGINIE: Madam knows the shopkeepers won't give any more credit.

MME MERCADET: I understand.

JUSTIN: The creditors are behind it all. I'd like to get even with them!

MME MERCADET: The best way would be to pay them!

JUSTIN: Wouldn't they be surprised!

THÉRÈSE: And unhappy! ...They wouldn't know what to do with their time.

MME MERCADET: There's no need to hide from you the great anxiety my husband's business dealings have caused me. We shall probably need your discretion. We can depend on you, can't we?

SERVANTS: Ah, madam!

MME MERCADET: All the master wants is to gain time, his mind is so full of ideas! ...Follow my instructions closely.

THÉRÈSE: Yes, madam! Virginie and I would go through fire for you!..

VIRGINIE: I was just saying what good employers we have and in their prosperity they'll remember how we behaved when they were in trouble.

JUSTIN: As for me, so long as I have enough to live on, I shall serve the master. I'm fond of him and I'm sure the day his business improves, we'll all profit by it.

(MERCADET *appears.)*

MME MERCADET: He's bound to give you a position in his first solid enterprise... all it needs is one last effort. Dear me! we mustn't let our temporary difficulties be known, a rich match is in store for Mam'selle Julie.

THÉRÈSE: Mam'selle deserves to be happy, poor girl! She's so good, so educated, so well bred.

VIRGINIE: Such talent! A regular nightingale!

JUSTIN: It's a crime to deprive a young lady of all her armaments, to withhold dresses and hats. Thérèse, you let them get away with it! If Madam is willing to give me the suitor's name, I'll go to all the tradesmen, I'll hint that I can send them this Monsieur...Monsieur...

MME MERCADET: De la Brive.

JUSTIN: Monsieur de la Brive to pay for the trousseau, then they'll deliver it...

THÉRÈSE: Madam never said anything to me about this marriage, otherwise I would have got it all, for Justin's plan's a good one...

VIRGINIE: Sure thing, they'll fall for it.

MME MERCADET: And they won't lose a penny.

MERCADET: *(Undertone to his wife)* Is this any way to talk to your servants! Tomorrow they'll be impertinent. *(To* JUSTIN*)* Justin, go at once to Monsieur Verdelin and ask him to come and see me about a business matter that brooks no delay! Assume an air of mystery to make sure he comes. —You, Thérèse, go back to Madame Mercadet's tradesmen and tell them pointblank that they must send the things your mistresses have ordered, they will be paid...yes, paid...in cash. Go!

*(*JUSTIN *and* THÉRÈSE *exit.)*

MERCADET: *(To* VIRGINIE*)* Now then! Has madam given you her orders?

VIRGINIE: No, sir.

MERCADET: You have to do yourself proud today! We are going to have four guests to dinner: Verdelin and his wife, Monsieur de Méricourt and Monsieur de la Brive. So there will be seven at table. Such dinners make the reputation of great cooks! To follow the soup, a splendid fish, then four entrèes, very delicately composed…

VIRGINIE: Sir!

MERCADET: For the next course…

VIRGINIE: Sir, the tradesmen…

MERCADET: What! Talking tradesmen the day my daughter and her intended are to meet?

VIRGINIE: They won't provide provisions.

MERCADET: You must go to their competitors, give them my custom, and they'll tip you for it.

VIRGINIE: But the ones I'm dropping, how will I pay them?

MERCADET: Don't worry about that! That's their worry!

VIRGINIE: And what if they demand to be paid by me? Oh, first off, I won't cover the costs…

MERCADET: *(Undertone to his wife)* This girl has money! *(Aloud)* Virginie, nowadays credit is the lifeblood of a government's finances. If my tradesmen fail to understand the laws of their own country and don't stop harassing me, they're unconstitutional radicals! Don't bother about people who rebel against the fundamental principle of all nations…the well-ordered ones! …Concern yourself with dinner, that's your duty! Show yourself to be a world-class cook! If Madame Mercadet, in settling accounts with you the day after my daughter's wedding, finds she owes you…I'll take care of it all!

VIRGINIE: Sir…

MERCADET: Besides, I can help you earn good interest, twenty percent annually!—and that's somewhat better than the savings bank…

VIRGINIE: They barely give one percent a year!

MERCADET: *(To* MME MERCADET*)* Didn't I tell you! *(To* VIRGINIE*)* What! You put your money in the hands of strangers? You're clever enough to invest it on your own and here your little nest-egg will never leave you.

VIRGINIE: *(Aside)* Twenty percent a year, goodness... *(Aloud)* Madam will advise me about the rest of the meal. I'll go and make lunch. *(Exits)*

MERCADET: *(Watching* VIRGINIE *as she goes out)* That girl has a thousand crowns in the savings bank... that she pilfered from us ...So now it's all quiet on the servant front...

MME MERCADET: Oh! sir, how can you stoop so low!

MERCADET: You never cease to amaze me! ...You with your well-organized little existence, without a care in the world, swaddled in comforts, out every night to the play or a soiree with our friend Méricourt, you...

MME MERCADET: But you asked him to escort me...

MERCADET: A man can't look after his wife and his business. In short, you play the elegant beauty...

MME MERCADET: You ordered me to!

MERCADET: Of course, it's imperative! A wife is a promoter's shop sign... When you show up at the opera sporting a new necklace, the audience says "asphalt must be a solid investment or mortgage guarantees have gone up, for Madame Mercadet looks so elegant...They're a lucky couple!" God willing, if my scheme for buying substitutes for military recruits is approved by the Minister of War you'll have a carriage!..

MME MERCADET: Sir, you can't think I am indifferent to your cares, your struggles and your honor?

MERCADET: Then don't criticize the means to my end. Just now, you were trying to coax your servants by kindness. You have to command…short and sharp, like Napoleon.

MME MERCADET: Order them about when you don't pay them!..

MERCADET: Precisely! You pay them with a bold front.

MME MERCADET: Sometimes you can win by kindness favors they would refuse a…

MERCADET: Kindness! Ah! Little do you know the age we're living in! Today, madam, fine feeling is on the way out, elbowed aside by money. Self-interest is everything, because there are no more families, only individuals. Look, everyone's future is in stocks and bonds! When a young woman needs a dowry she no longer turns to her family, but to a mutual fund. The king of England's inheritance is invested in an insurance company. The wife depends not on her husband, but on the savings and loan! Debts are paid to the nation through a sort of white-slave trade, buying substitutes for military draftees! All our obligations are settled by clipping coupons! We change our servants as often as we change our title-deeds, so they're no longer devoted to their employers. Hold on to their money and they will serve you well!

MME MERCADET: Oh, sir, you so honorable, so upright, sometimes you say things that make me–

MERCADET: And what I say I may also do, right?.. Well! I would do anything to keep afloat, for *(He pulls out a five-franc piece.)* this is modern honor! …Sell plaster of Paris as sugar. If you can make a fortune without being hauled into court, you become a member of parliament, a peer of France or a cabinet minister! Do you know why plays whose heroes are con-men are so popular?.. It's because the audience pats itself on the back and says, "At any rate I'm better than those scoundrels!" As for me I have an excuse. I bear the burden of Godeau's crime. And anyway, what's so dishonorable about being in debt? ...Every government in Europe has debts. Doesn't every man die in debt to his father? He owes him life and cannot pay it back. The earth is constantly bankrupted by the sun. Life, madam, is perpetual borrowing! Just try not to borrow! Am I not superior to my creditors? I've got their money while they're still waiting for mine. I ask nothing of them yet they keep pestering me! A man who owes nothing matters to no one, whereas my creditors take a keen interest in me!

MME MERCADET: A little too much! ...Owing and repaying is all very well, but owing and being unable to repay, borrowing when you know you're incapable of discharging the debt! I don't dare tell you what I think of that.

MERCADET: You think matters are beginning to...

MME MERCADET: I'm afraid...

MERCADET: So you no longer have faith in me, your...

MME MERCADET: I still have faith in you, but I'm in despair when I see you eaten up by efforts that fall short. I admire the fertility of your ideas, but I grieve when I have to hear the paradoxes you use to numb yourself.

MERCADET: A melancholic man would have drowned himself by now! A ton of depression doesn't pay two pennysworth of debts... Come, come! can you tell me where honesty begins or ends in the business world? Look...we have no money at all... need I say so?

MME MERCADET: Certainly not.

MERCADET: Is that swindling? Nobody would give me a penny if they knew it! Well then! Don't condemn the means I use to keep my seat at the great gaming table of speculation by making people believe in my financial prowess. All credit implies deceit! So you must help me hide our destitution behind a dazzling show of luxury. Scenery is worked by machines and machines get dirty! Don't worry, many a man who might turn up his nose has done worse. Louis XIV, when in financial straits, personally showed off his hunting lodge to the banker Bernard to obtain several millions, and nowadays modern laws have led us all to say with him: I am the government!

MME MERCADET: So long as, while in financial straits, you preserve your honor. You know, sir, you don't have to justify yourself to me...

MERCADET: You show a great deal of sympathy for my creditors, but we owe them money because of...

MME MERCADET: Their confidence in us!

MERCADET: Their greed! The speculator and the investor are one and the same! They both want to get rich quick. I have done all my creditors a favor. They all expect to get something out of me! I'd be lost if I didn't have intimate knowledge of their selfish interests and their private passions, so I make each of them play out his little comedy!

MME MERCADET: I'm worried about the final curtain! Some of them are sick and tired of playing along. Goulard, for instance. What can you do against such ferocity, he'll force you to file a petition in bankruptcy...

MERCADET: Over my dead body! The gold mines aren't in Mexico any more, they're at the stock market! and I intend to stay there until I uncover my vein of ore!...

(*Enter* GOULARD)

GOULARD: I'm delighted to find you in, my dear sir.

MME MERCADET: *(Aside)* Heavens, it's Goulard. What is he going to do? *(To* MERCADET*)* Auguste!

(MERCADET *signals to* MME MERCADET *to keep calm.)*

GOULARD: This is a rare sighting, one has to catch you in the morning and take advantage of when the door is open and the keepers are away.

MERCADET: Keepers! Are we animals in the zoo? You're unparalleled!

GOULARD: No, I'm unpaid, Monsieur Mercadet.

MERCADET: Monsieur Goulard!

GOULARD: I won't be fobbed off with words.

MERCADET: I know, You need actions, transactions, and I can offer you plenty in payment…I'm a share-holder in…

GOULARD: No jokes, I've come intending to put an end to this…

MME MERCADET: Put an end to it…no, sir, I can offer you my…

MERCADET: My dear, let Monsieur Goulard have his say.

*(*GOULARD *bows to* MME MERCADET.*)*

MERCADET: You're in your own home, hear him out!

GOULARD: Sorry, madam, I'm delighted you're here, for your co-signing might…

MERCADET: It is wrong of my wife to meddle in our conversation, women know nothing of business! *(To his wife)* This gentleman is my creditor, my dear. He's come to claim the sum total of his loans, capital, interest and costs, for you haven't treated me kindly, Goulard… Ah!, you've roughly persecuted a man with whom you've had done so much business.

GOULARD: Business which hasn't always turned a profit for me.

MERCADET: What would be the merit in that? If business resulted in nothing but profit, everyone would be at it!

GOULARD: I didn't come here so you could show off how clever you are! ...I know you're cleverer than I am, because you've got my money...

MERCADET: Well, money has to be somewhere! *(To* MME MERCADET*)* This is a gentleman who has hunted me down like a hare! Come, admit it, my dear Goulard, you've behaved badly! Anybody but me would take his revenge now, for I can cause you to lose a huge sum of money.

GOULARD: I can believe that if you go on not paying me, but you will or tomorrow I'll turn over your bills to the authorities.

MERCADET: Oh! never mind what I owe you, you need have no anxiety on that score, nor need I. More important capital is at stake! I'm stupefied to see you, a man with so keen a vision, such sound advice, involved in that swindle! ...You! ...But then, we all have moments when we make a wrong move...

GOULARD: What are you talking about?

MERCADET: *(To his wife)* You would never believe... *(To* GOULARD*)* She does know a thing or two about speculations, she has a knack for assessing them!... *(To his wife)* Well, my dear, Goulard's in it for a very considerable amount.

MME MERCADET: Sir?

GOULARD: *(Aside)* This Mercadet has a genius for speculation. Is he fooling? *(To* MERCADET*)* What do you mean? What's this all about?

MERCADET: You know! ...You always know where the shoe pinches, when you own stock.

GOULARD: You're referring to the Basse-Indre mines? It's a once-in-a-lifetime opportunity...

MERCADET: Once in a lifetime? ...Yes, for those who sold out yesterday.

GOULARD: Some investors sold out?

MERCADET: In secret, insider trading! You'll see it plummet today and tomorrow...especially tomorrow when it goes public...

GOULARD: Thanks, Mercadet, we'll discuss our little business later. Madam, my respects...

MERCADET: Hold on, my dear Goulard! *(He tugs* GOULARD *by the arm.)* I have some news that will reassure you...

GOULARD: What about?

MERCADET: About your loans! I'm marrying off my daughter...

GOULARD: *(Pulling away)* Later...

MERCADET: *(Grabbing him again)* No, right now, he's a millionaire...

GOULARD: Congratulations... Oh! that mine! My best wishes! ...You can count on me.

MME MERCADET: For the wedding?

GOULARD: *(Pulling away again)* Absolutely.

MERCADET: Listen! One more word...

GOULARD: No, good-bye. Good luck in that business.

*(*MERCADET *brings* GOULARD *back with a gesture:)*

MERCADET: If you want to give me some securities, I'll tell you how you can sell your shares to...

GOULARD: My dear Mercadet! We'll come to an understanding.

MERCADET: *(To his wife)* You see how ready he is to rob his neighbor? Is that a man of honor?

GOULARD: Well?

MERCADET: Do you have my promissory notes on you?

GOULARD: No.

MERCADET: Then what are you going to do?

GOULARD: I'm going to find out just what shape you're in.

MERCADET: As you see.

GOULARD: Delighted. Goodbye.

*(*MERCADET *follows* GOULARD *out, trying to hold him back.)*

MME MERCADET: *(Alone for a moment)* It's a miracle.

MERCADET: *(Returns, laughing)* Impossible to keep him here! He turned his back on me like a drunk at a water fountain.

MME MERCADET: *(Laughs as well)* Were you telling him the truth? I couldn't figure out what you were saying…

MERCADET: It was in the interest of my friend Verdelin. He's contriving a panic in Basse-Indre shares, a risky venture that's suddenly become a gilt-edged investment. *(Aside)* If Verdelin succeeds in quashing it, I'll get involved… *(Aloud)* That brings us to the main event, Julie's marriage! Yes, now I need a second self to reap what I've sown.

MME MERCADET: Ah, sir, if you'd taken me as your cashier, today we'd have thirty thousand francs a year!

MERCADET: The day I have thirty thousand francs a year, I'll be a ruined man. Think about it! If you had had your way, we'd be buried in the provinces with the few pennies left after the involuntary loan we made that monster Godeau. Then where would we be? Would you have met that Méricourt you're so fond of and whom you've made your prince consort? That social butterfly, which is what he is, is going to get Julie off our hands! The poor girl is not our finest product.

MME MERCADET: Some men of sense think beauty is fleeting...

MERCADET: There are men of better sense who think ugliness is lasting.

MME MERCADET: Julie is loving...

MERCADET: I'm not her intended! I know my role as father! I'm a bit surprised by this young man's sudden passion, I'd like to know what he finds so charming about my daughter.

MME MERCADET: Julie's voice is charming, she's musical.

MERCADET: He may be one of our less discerning dilettantes, for I believe he goes in for comic opera and doesn't know a word of Italian.

MME MERCADET: Julie's educated...

MERCADET: You mean she reads novels. And doesn't write them, which proves she's an intelligent girl. Let's hope Julie, for all her reading, will understand marriage the right way, as a business deal! We've left her to her own devices for the last two years. She's grown up so much!

MME MERCADET: Poor child! She's so well acquainted with the secret of our situation that she learned a skill, painting on china, so she wouldn't be a burden to us...

MERCADET: You didn't fulfill your obligations to her. *(Mme Mercadet winces.)* You were supposed to make her pretty.

MME MERCADET: She's better than that, she's virtuous.

MERCADET: Intelligent and virtuous! What more could a husband ask?

MME MERCADET: Sir!

MERCADET: In the way of accomplishments! Go and get her, for we have to explain the reason for tonight's dinner and urge her to take Monsieur de la Brive seriously.

MME MERCADET: The problems with the tradesmen kept me from speaking to her yesterday. I'll bring Julie here. She's awake, because she gets up at first light to paint. *(She exits.)*

MERCADET: These days to marry off a young and beautiful daughter, to marry her off well as we understand it, is a rather tricky problem to solve. But to marry off a daughter of questionable looks whose only dowry is her virtue, I ask the most scheming mothers, isn't that a hell of a job? Méricourt must be very fond of us. My wife still makes of him what she will, which reassures me... Yes, perhaps he feels obliged to find an advantageous match for Julie. As for the fiancé, Monsieur de la Brive, just to see him lashing his horse on the Champs-Èlysées, the style of his groom, the look of his carriage, his deportment at the opera, the most demanding father would be satisfied. I dined at his home: a charming apartment, solid silverware, an ormolu dessert service with his coat of arms, so it wasn't borrowed. What woman could tempt a leading light of the gilded youth to get married?.. For he's been successful with the ladies... Oh, perhaps he's weary of such success... And Méricourt told me he'd heard Julie sing exquisitely at the Duvals'... At long last, my daughter is making a good marriage. But is he?...

*(*MME MERCADET *and* JULIE *enter.)*

MME MERCADET: Julie, your father and I have something to say on a subject a young lady always likes to hear. You will be meeting your intended. You may be about to be married, my child…

JULIE: Why may be? It must be a sure thing.

MERCADET: Girls about to be married never have doubts.

JULIE: Has Monsieur Minard spoken to you, father?

MERCADET: Monsieur Minard! …Eh! …What is a Monsieur Minard? …Did you expect, madam, to find a Monsieur Minard ensconced in your daughter's heart? Julie, would he by chance be that junior clerk Duval, my ex-cashier, often suggested I hire? A poor fellow who knows only his mother… *(Aside)* Godeau's illegitimate son… *(To* JULIE*)* Answer me!

JULIE: Yes, papa.

MERCADET: Do you love him?

JULIE: Yes, papa.

MERCADET: Loving's not enough, you have to be loved back.

MME MERCADET: Does he love you?

JULIE: Yes, mama!

MERCADET: "Yes, papa. Yes, mama", why not dada and nana? Girls may be well over the age of consent, but they talk as if they've just been weaned! …Do your mother the favor of calling her Madam while she still enjoys the bloom of youth and beauty.

JULIE: Yes, sir.

MERCADET: Oh! you may call me father, it won't bother me! What proof do you have he loves you?

JULIE: Well…I feel loved!

MERCADET: But what proof do you have?

JULIE: The best of proofs, he wants to marry me.

MERCADET: It's true! These girls, like toddlers, completely disarm you with their answers.

MME MERCADET: Where did you see him?

JULIE: Here.

MME MERCADET: When?

JULIE: At night, after you'd gone out.

MME MERCADET: He's younger than you…

JULIE: By a few months!

MME MERCADET: And you thought it entirely reasonable that a young scatterbrain of twenty-two is able to appreciate your qualities.

JULIE: But he noticed me first. If I had loved him first, I never would have let him know. We met at an evening party at Madame Duval's.

MME MERCADET: Madame Duval makes a specialty of inviting nobodies!

MERCADET: She runs a salon, she wants dancers at all costs! …People who dance have no future! Today young men with ambition act serious and don't dance.

JULIE: Adolphe…

MERCADET: And his name's Adolphe!.. And imbeciles insist that the world is making progress. They take upheaval for improvement. Is the world still turning? Children trust less than ever in their fathers' experience… Be advised, mam'selle, that a clerk with a salary of twelve hundred francs does not know the meaning of love, he hasn't got the time, he has to work too hard. Only landowners, men with smart carriages, in short, loafers can know how to love.

MME MERCADET: But, you wretched child!..

MERCADET: *(To his wife)* Let me talk to her. *(To* JULIE*)* Julie, I'll marry you to your Monsieur Minard.

(JULIE *makes a gesture.)*

MERCADET: Hold on! You haven't got a penny to your name, you know. What's to become of you the day after your wedding? Have you thought about that?

JULIE: Yes, father..

MME MERCADET: She's gone crazy!

MERCADET: *(To his wife)* She's in love, poor girl!...Let her have her say. *(To* JULIE*)* Tell me all about it, Julie, I'm not your father now, I'm your closest friend and I'm listening.

JULIE: We love one another.

MERCADET: But will Cupid shoot you dividends on the tips of his arrows?

JULIE: Oh, father! We'll live in a small apartment in a remote part of town, on the top floor, if need be! If I have to, I'll be his maid... Ah! I'll do the housework with infinite pleasure, dreaming that this, like everything else, is for his sake ...I'll work for him while he's working for me! I'll keep trouble from coming near him, he'll never know how hard-up we are. Our household will be clean, even elegant. Goodness me! Elegance is easy to achieve, it issues from the soul and happiness is both its cause and effect. I can earn enough with my china painting to cost him nothing and even contribute to our budget. Besides, love will see us through the hard times! ...Adolphe is ambitious like all men with lofty souls and he will be a success...

MERCADET: A bachelor may become a success, but a married man wears himself out paying bills and running after a thousand francs the way a dog runs after a carriage. So he's ambitious?

JULIE: Father, Adolphe has so much will-power and ability that I'm sure one day he'll be…a cabinet minister, why not?

MERCADET: Nowadays, who doesn't fancy himself a cabinet minister, at the very least? On leaving school, they think they'll be a great poet, a great public speaker, a great minister, like under Napoleon, every second lieutenant dreamt of being a field marshal. You know what your Adolphe will be? Father of a horde of children who will wreck your plans of working and saving, who will put his Excellency in debtor's prison and who will plunge you into appalling poverty! You've been describing the romance, not the history, of life.

MME MERCADET: Poor child! At her age, it's easy to take hopes for realities!..

MERCADET: She thinks love is the only factor in marital bliss. She's wrong, like all those who attribute their own blunders to chance, the editor responsible for our typographical errors! And then they lay the blame on society after they've turned it upside-down. Bah! This is a passing fancy with no serious basis.

JULIE: But, father, we're both willing to sacrifice everything to this love.

MME MERCADET: What! Julie, wouldn't you sacrifice this new-born love to save your father? To restore the life he gave you, the honor that families must keep intact!

MERCADET: What's the use of the romance novels you've been wallowing in, you wretched child, if you haven't imbibed a desire to imitate the obedience they preach? (For novels have become social sermons!) Does your Adolphe know the state of your fortune? Have you painted for him your idyllic life on the top floor, with trees up against your window and cherries for dinner, like Rousseau with his barmaid?

JULIE: Father, I would never make an indiscreet remark that might compromise you.

MERCADET: He thinks we're rich?

JULIE: He's never spoken to me about money.

MERCADET: *(Aside, to his wife)* Right, now I've got it. *(To* JULIE*)* Julie, write to him at once to come and see me.

JULIE: *(Kissing him)* Ah, father!

MERCADET: This very day an elegant young man with a noble name, a leading light of high society, is coming to dine here. This young man has intentions and takes an interest in you. That's our candidate. You will not be Madame Minard, but Madame de la Brive. Instead of climbing to the top floor in a slum, you will have a fine house on the finest avenue. You have talent, education, you could play a brilliant role in Paris. If you're not the wife of a cabinet minister, you may be the wife of a peer of France. I'm sorry, daughter, I have nothing better to offer you...

JULIE: Don't tease me about my love, father, let me simply accept happiness and poverty rather than unhappiness and riches.

MME MERCADET: Julie, your father and I are responsible for your future, and we don't want you some day to have good reason to complain of us, for the parents' experience should be a lesson for the children. At the moment life is treating us cruelly. Come, daughter, marry riches.

MERCADET: In this case, the majority is right! That's the motto of money in this Republic.

MME MERCADET: Happiness is impossible in poverty, but there's no unhappiness riches cannot assuage.

JULIE: How can you, my mother, say such depressing things! Father, I'm going to speak your bitter and material language. Haven't I heard you talk of rich, idle people who are helpless when they are eventually faced with misfortune, ruined by their vices or their carelessness, plunging their families into irreparable misery? Wouldn't it be better to marry a poor girl to a man without a fortune, though capable of earning one. Monsieur de la Brive may, for all I know, be rich, clever and highly talented, but so were you. You lost your fortune and took as my mother a rich, beautiful girl, whereas I…

MERCADET: Daughter, you'll be able to judge Monsieur de la Brive as I shall judge Monsieur Minard. But you'll have no choice. Monsieur Minard will give you up himself.

JULIE: Oh! never, father, he'll win your heart.

MME MERCADET: My dear, what if he does love her?

MERCADET: He's toying with her.

JULIE: I want nothing better than to be toyed with that way.

MME MERCADET: Someone's ringing! and there's no one to open the door.

MERCADET: Then let 'em ring.

MME MERCADET: I keep thinking that Godeau may be back.

MERCADET: Godeau! …Remember that with his principles of making a fortune, *quibuscumque viis*… (look at that! I'm speaking Latin), any which way, Godeau may have been keelhauled from a yardarm. After eight years with no news, you're still waiting for Godeau! You remind me of those old soldiers who keep expecting the return of Napoleon.

MME MERCADET: There goes the bell again!

MERCADET: That's the way a creditor rings! ...Julie, go and see who it is. And, whatever they say tell them your mother and I are out. If this creditor has any shame, he'll believe an innocent young lady...

(JULIE *exits.*)

MME MERCADET: This love is sincere at least on her side, and it touched me.

MERCADET: You women are all romantics!

MME MERCADET: A first love makes one strong!...

MERCADET: Strong enough to go into debt! And it's bad enough that the father-in-law...

JULIE: *(Returns)* It's Monsieur Pierquin, father!

MERCADET: So the young guard has been defeated!

JULIE: But he insists it's about a good business deal for you.

MERCADET: For him, he means. That she lets her Adolphe talk her round is only natural, but a creditor! I know how to deal with this fellow! Leave us alone!

*(The women withdraw.* PIERQUIN *enters.)*

PIERQUIN: I didn't come to ask for money, my dear sir, I know you're arranging a splendid marriage. Your daughter is marrying a millionaire, the news is already going round.

MERCADET: Oh, a millionaire...where'd you hear that! He's well-to-do...

PIERQUIN: This magnificent prospect will help appease your creditors. Personally, I've withdrawn the complaint I put before the Board of Trade.

MERCADET: Were you thinking of having me arrested?

PIERQUIN: Ah! you've had a two years' grace period! I never let a promissory note go for so long, but for you, I set aside my principles. If this marriage is a hoax, I congratulate you…Godeau's return was getting damnably stale! …A son-in-law will give you time. Ah, my dear fellow, the merry chase you've led us with these expectations would puzzle a farce writer! Dear me! I am fond of you, you're so ingenious! A rich husband for a girl without a dowry, that's bold.

MERCADET: *(Aside)* What's he getting at?

PIERQUIN: Goulard swallowed the hook, but what did you bait it with? He's a shrewd one.

MERCADET: My son-in-law Monsieur de la Brive is a young man…

PIERQUIN: So there's a real young man?

MERCADET: I can show him to you…

PIERQUIN: How much are you paying the young man?

MERCADET: Enough of this insolence! Otherwise, my dear sir, I shall demand a settling of accounts; and, my dear Monsieur Pierquin, you will lose a good deal of the price at which you sell me your money!

PIERQUIN: Sir!

MERCADET: I'm going to be so rich that I won't have to put up with anyone's sarcasm, not even a creditor's. What business have you come to propose?

PIERQUIN: If you want to settle up, I'd like that every bit as much…

MERCADET: I don't believe it. I bring you in as much as a productive farm.

PIERQUIN: I was coming to offer you a term of payment by securities, for which I'll grant you a postponement of three months.

MERCADET: Is it a lucrative deal?

PIERQUIN: Yes.

MERCADET: *(Aside)* What has this fox sniffed out? geese with golden eggs. *(Aloud)* Explain yourself clearly.

PIERQUIN: You know me, I'm lucid, limpid, crystal clear.

MERCADET: No phrasemaking! I've never given you a hard time for being a loan shark, for I consider heavy interest to be a bonus on the capital of a business deal. A loan shark is a capitalist who takes his profits in advance…

PIERQUIN: Look, here are bills of exchange worth fifty thousand francs, from a very pretty young man named Michonnin, a slippery character…

MERCADET: Who slipped away…

PIERQUIN: Yes. It's all in order: complaint of non-payment, judgment of default, final judgment, report of arrears, arrest warrant, et cetera, et cetera…there are five thousand francs in costs to be paid

MERCADET: And it's worth?

PIERQUIN: It's worth the future of a young man who is now forced to be very ingenious to go on living.

MERCADET: In other words, it's worthless.

PIERQUIN: Unless he marries a wealthy Englishwoman, in love with…

MERCADET: Him?

PIERQUIN: No, a title! And I was thinking of buying him one… But that would have involved me in government red tape.

MERCADET: What do you want of me?

PIERQUIN: Something of equal non-value.

MERCADET: What?

PIERQUIN: Shares in…well, those of your enterprises that no longer pay dividends.

MERCADET: And you'll grant me a postponement of five months?

PIERQUIN: No, three months.

MERCADET: *(Aside)* Three months! For a speculator, that's an eternity! But what's on his mind? Oh! nothing ventured, nothing gained. *(Aloud)* Pierquin, despite my brilliant mind, I fail to understand you, but I'm with you…

PIERQUIN: I was counting on it! Here's a letter granting you the postponement. Here're the Michonnin papers. Ah, you should know: this young man has worn out every process-server in Paris.

MERCADET: Would you like pink stocks for a newspaper which might be successful if it ever appeared? blue stocks for a mine that blew up? yellow stocks for paving stones that can't be made into barricades?..

PIERQUIN: Give me every color you've got.

MERCADET: Here you are, my dear colleague, forty thousand francs' worth.

PIERQUIN: Thank you, dear friend! Our sort knows how to make things hum.

MERCADET: *(Aside)* His theme song whenever he's pulled something off! I've been robbed. *(Aloud)* You're going to offer my stocks?

PIERQUIN: Of course.

MERCADET: At full value?

PIERQUIN: If possible…

MERCADET: Ah! now I get it! This new collateral replaces your cases of stuffed animals, your ships in bottles, your sable coats, your whole fantastic inventory…

PIERQUIN: It's got so old!..

MERCADET: And besides the courts are beginning to find them flimsy… Ah! You are a righteous man, you are going to breathe new life into my stocks.

PIERQUIN: Believe me, my dear friend, I would like to!

MERCADET: Wouldn't I? Goodbye!

PIERQUIN: You have my best wishes, as a creditor, for your daughter's wedding. *(He exits.)*

MERCADET: *(Alone)* Michonnin! Forty-two thousand francs and five thousand in interest and costs, forty-seven thousand… No payment on account! Bah! a man worth nothing today might become top drawer tomorrow! Besides, I'll promote him to baron when I interest certain parties in a lucrative deal! Well, well, well! …My wife knows an Englishwoman who puts shells and algae on her head, daughter of a brewer and… Damn! No permanent address…let's not find fault with the unfortunate fellow! Do I know if I'll have a place to live in three months? Poor boy! Perhaps, like me, he too had a partner! Everyone has his Godeau, a phony Christopher Columbus! After all, Godeau… *(He looks around to see if he's alone.)* I do believe Godeau has already brought me in more money than he took from me!

END OF ACT ONE

# ACT TWO

*(*MERCADET *rings for* JUSTIN, *who enters:)*

MERCADET: What did Verdelin, my friend Verdelin, have to say?

JUSTIN: He'll be here soon, by a lucky chance he has money to give to Monsieur Brédif.

MERCADET: Make sure that he talks to me before going to Brédif's. Ah! …I gave a hundred francs to old Grumeau the concierge, he can't have told two lies in twenty-four hours for just a hundred francs.

JUSTIN: Especially, sir, as I made him think he was telling the truth.

MERCADET: You'll end up becoming my secretary…

JUSTIN: Ah! if only I knew how to write!…

MERCADET: Secretaries of cabinet ministers write very little.

JUSTIN: What do they do then?

MERCADET: Housework! And they speak when their boss has to keep his mouth shut… Anyway, fix it so that old Grumeau tells Verdelin that Brédif has gone out.

*(Exit* JUSTIN.*)*

MERCADET: *(Aside)* That fellow is half a Figaro, for nowadays full-fledged Figaros become our masters! …

Our social climbers these days are unemployed valets who feather their nests in France!

*(Enter* THÉRÈSE *and* VIRGINIE.*)*

MERCADET: Well, Thérèse!

THÉRÈSE: Sir, the minute I promised to pay, all the tradesmen broke into smiles…

MERCADET: The smile of a salesman who's made a sale!… *( To* VIRGINIE*)* And shall we have a fine dinner, Virginie?

VIRGINIE: The proof of the pudding's in the eating!

MERCADET: And the suppliers?

VIRGINIE: Bah! They agree to wait!

MERCADET: *(Aside)* She paid them herself. *(Aloud)* I won't forget it. I'll settle with you tomorrow…

VIRGINIE: If Mam'selle gets married, she'll probably keep me in mind.

MERCADET: What d'ye mean, if! The marriage is a sure thing.

*(Exit* VIRGINIE.*)*

THÉRÈSE: What about me, sir?

MERCADET: I'll find you a husband among one of the future employees of my company for insuring against the risk of being drafted. But…

THÉRÈSE: Don't worry, sir. I know what to say to a suitor to make him madly in love and to make him as cool as an ice-house…I had revenge on my last mistress by getting her to break off her marriage…

MERCADET: Ah, a chamber-maid's tattle! It's a do-it-yourself thriller…

THÉRÈSE: Oh! sir, we don't have that much…talent! *(She exits.)*

MERCADET: *(Alone)* Having your servants on your side is like a government with the press behind it! Fortunately mine have their wages to lose. Now everything relies on the dubious friendship of Verdelin, a man whose fortune is my doing! But to rail at man's ingratitude you'd have to be a Martin Luther of the heart. As soon as a man turns forty, he ought to know the world is peopled with ingrates! I really have no idea where the benefactors are hiding! ...Verdelin and I have great respect for one another. He owes me gratitude, I owe him money, and neither of us pays the other! ...Come now! to marry off Julie, I've got to find a thousand crowns in a pocket that pretends to be empty! To break into a heart so as to break into a strong-box, what a project! ...Only women who are loved can pull off such stunts!

JUSTIN: *(Entering)* Monsieur Verdelin is here.

*(*VIOLETTE *enters.)*

MERCADET: Here he is...my friend... Oh, it's old Violette... *(To* JUSTIN*)* Eleven years working for me and you still don't know how to keep a door closed? Go on, keep an eye out for Verdelin and banter with him until I've got rid of this poor devil.

JUSTIN: One of his victims. *(He exits.)*

VIOLETTE: This is my eleventh visit this week, my dear Monsieur Mercadet, and necessity drove me to wait for you three hours in the street yesterday, on my way from here to the Stock Exchange. I see I was told the truth when they swore you were in the country.

MERCADET: We're both hard up, poor old Violette! We both have families...

VIOLETTE: We've pawned all we can...

MERCADET: So have we...

VIOLETTE: One man's misery can't cure another's... You still have enough to live on while we haven't a crumb! I never reproached you for my ruin, for I believe it was your intention to make me rich... and besides, it was my own fault! I wanted to double my little fortune and I compromised it. My wife and my daughters, who urged me to speculate, who scolded me for my timidity, can't understand that to seize the chance to make a lot of money is to expose oneself to losing just as much... Still, words butter no parsnips. I'm here to implore you to give me the tiniest bit of the interest on account. You'll be saving the life of a whole family.

MERCADET: *(Aside)* Poor fellow, he's breaking my heart! ...Whenever I see him, I lose my appetite!... *(Aloud)* Be reasonable, I'll go shares with you... We have barely a hundred francs in the house... and even that is my daughter's money.

VIOLETTE: Can it be!.. You, Monsieur Mercadet, who was once so rich!

MERCADET: Fellows in distress owe each other the truth.

VIOLETTE: If that were all they owed, how prompt would be the payment!

MERCADET: Don't press me! ...For I am just about to marry off my daughter...

VIOLETTE: I have two daughters, sir, and they work with no hope of being married, for women who hold on to their virtue earn so little! ...Given your circumstances, I won't plead with you, but...my wife and daughters await my return in fear and trembling... At my age, there's nothing I can do...unless you... could find me a position.

MERCADET: You're on the list, dear old Violette, you will be cashier at my company for insuring against the risk of….

VIOLETTE: Ah! my wife and daughters will bless you!…

(MERCADET *goes to get some money.)*

VIOLETTE: The others hound him and get nothing, but by a little whining, I'll have my interest back bit by bit…

MERCADET: Here's sixty francs!

VIOLETTE: In gold! It's been a long time since I've seen the like… When I get home!…

MERCADET: But…

VIOLETTE: Don't worry, I won't say a word…

MERCADET: That's not it. Promise me, dear old Violette, not to come back here for…a month…

VIOLETTE: A month! Can we live a month on this?

MERCADET: That's all you have?

VIOLETTE: My only money is what you owe me…

MERCADET: Poor fellow, the sight of him make me feel rich. *(Aloud)* I thought you were doing a little business lending money in the financial district?

VIOLETTE: Ever since the imprisoned debtors were let out of jail, lending has hit rock bottom in that neighborhood.

MERCADET: Could you acquire the security to get a cashier's job?

VIOLETTE: I have a couple of friends, and maybe…

MERCADET: Would they accept stocks?

VIOLETTE: Oh, sir, you wheeler-dealers, you busted the main spring of mutual societies! No one wants to hear about stocks any more…

MERCADET: Too bad. Goodbye, Violette old man! We'll settle up another time...You'll be the first to be paid...

VIOLETTE: Good luck, sir! My wife and daughters will say prayers for the marriage of Mam'selle Mercadet. *(He exits.)*

MERCADET: Goodbye! If all my creditors were like him, I wouldn't have a leg to stand on, he always wrings money out of me

*(*VERDELIN *enters.)*

VERDELIN: Good afternoon, my friend. What's up?

MERCADET: Your question leaves me no time to sugar-coat the pill! You can figure it out!

VERDELIN: Oh, Mercadet old fellow, I haven't got it and I'll be frank. Even if I did I wouldn't give it to you! Listen: I've already lent you all that my means allow me to; I've never asked you for repayment. I'm your friend and your creditor. Well, if my heart weren't overflowing with gratitude, if I'd been the average man, the creditor would long ago have polished off the friend! ...For Chrissake! ...There's a limit to everything in this world!

MERCADET: Friendship, yes! ...But not bad luck!

VERDELIN: If I were rich enough to save you altogether, to cancel out your debt entirely, I'd do so with all my heart, for I admire your courage. But you're doomed to go under! Your latest schemes, ingenious, even plausible as they are (so many people fell for them) have collapsed, your reputation's in tatters, you're considered dangerous! You weren't able to profit by the temporary vogue for your enterprises! ...When you're down and out, you will always find a place at my table! ...It's a friend's duty to speak home truths!...

MERCADET: What would friendship be without the pleasure of being wise when we see our friend being foolish, of being comfortable when we see our friend ruined, of congratulating ourselves by speaking unpleasant home truths! …So, I'm condemned by public opinion?

VERDELIN: I wouldn't go that far. No, you're still considered an honorable man, but necessity is forcing you to go to extremes…

MERCADET: Which are not sanctified by success, unlike with lucky men. Ah, success! …How many infamous acts go to make up success you can judge for yourself… This morning I caused the fall in shares that you wanted so you could squash the Basse-Indre mine deal and gain control before the engineers' report goes public, thanks to the silence you sell so dearly.

VERDELIN: Hush! Mercadet, can this be true? I can see your hand at work… *(Puts his arm around his waist.)*

MERCADET: All this to make you understand I have no need of hugs or sermons, just money! For heaven's sake! I ask not for myself, good friend, but I'm marrying off my daughter, and we are, secretly, on the brink of poverty… Indigence reigns in this house for all the appearance of luxury (promises, credit, all used up!) And if I don't pay cash for certain indispensable expenses, this marriage will not come off! All I need now is two weeks of opulence, just as all you need is twenty-four hours to lie to the Stock Market. Verdelin, I shall never repeat this request. Must I say it! My wife and Julie haven't a new rag to their backs. *(Aside)* He's hesitating…

VERDELIN: *(Aside)* He's played me so many comedies I don't even know if his daughter is getting married! … How can she!

MERCADET: This very day I have to give a dinner to my son-in-law-to-be, who was introduced to us by a mutual friend, and I don't even have any silverware.

It's gone…you know where… Not only do I need a thousand crowns, but I also hope you'll lend me your dinner service and come to supper here with your wife,

VERDELIN: A thousand crowns!.. Mercadet!.. No one has a thousand crowns…to lend… A person barely has that much for himself! If a man were to lend money whenever he was asked, he would never have any…

MERCADET: *(Aside)* Oh, he'll cough up. *(Aloud)* Believe it or not, once my daughter is married, I don't care what happens. My wife will have a roof over her head with Julie and I shall seek my fortune somewhere else, for you're right about me. Useful to others I am deadly to myself! I may be magnificent in sowing the seeds of announcements and prospectuses, in understanding and satisfying the needs of an infant company, but I know nothing of harvesting…

VERDELIN: You want to know the answer to this riddle?

MERCADET: Tell me!..

VERDELIN: It's because your intelligence is superior to your judgment. The mind may win us admiration, but it's judgment that confers a fortune on us.

MERCADET: *(Aside)* Yes, I don't have enough judgment to crush a deal that will profit me! *(Aloud)* See here, Verdelin! …I love my wife and daughter… These feelings are my only consolation amid my recent disasters. These women have been so gentle, so patient! I'd like them to be beyond the reach of hardship! … Oh! that's what pains me so! …Don't be surprised a man can shed tears… *(He dabs his eyes.)* …You have a charming little girl, you wouldn't want her one day to be unhappy, growing old with tears and hard labor… But that is the future for my Julie, an angel of devotion! Oh! dear friend! Recently I have had to drink from a very bitter cup. I have slipped on my wooden sidewalks, I've organized monopolies and others stripped me of them! Ah well! this would be nothing compared to the pain of seeing you refuse me in this supreme emergency! However, let's not dwell on what comes next...for I wish to owe nothing to your pity!

VERDELIN: A thousand crowns! ...But what use will you make of them?

MERCADET: *(Aside)* It's in the bag! *(Aloud)* My dear fellow, a son-in-law is a bird easily frightened away... One bit of lace missing on a gown tells the sorry tale! The gowns were ordered, the tradesmen were about to deliver them... Yes, I was imprudent enough to say I'd pay cash, for I counted on you! ...And the dinner! It needs exquisite wines! ...That's the only way the suitor will lose his head. Pay close attention: we appear to be rich; we have to keep up appearances for Monsieur de la Brive! Verdelin! a thousand crowns won't kill you, you have sixty thousand francs a year! And you'll bring to life a poor girl you're fond of, for you are fond of Julie! ...She's crazy about your little girl, they play together like souls in bliss. Would you let your daughter's playmate wither on the vine? That sort of thing is catching, it brings bad luck!...

VERDELIN: My dear fellow, I haven't got a thousand crowns. I can lend you my dinner service, but I haven't got....

MERCADET: A draft on your bank is quickly signed...

VERDELIN: I... No...

MERCADET: Oh! my poor child!.. it's over and done with!... *(He collapses crushed into an armchair.)* God Almighty, forgive me if I end the painful dream of my existence and let me awake in Thy bosom!

VERDELIN: Have you really found a son-in-law, my friend?

MERCADET: *(Rising abruptly)* Have I found a son-in-law? …You actually doubt my word?.. Ah! You may cruelly refuse me the means of bringing about my daughter's happiness, but do not insult me! You shall see Monsieur de la Brive! …I've fallen so low that… Oh! Verdelin…I would not believe for a thousand crowns you could think such a thing of me! …You can never win my forgiveness except by giving them to me…

VERDELIN: I'll go and see if I can…

MERCADET: No! That's only another way of fobbing me off…

VERDELIN: But what if the marriage doesn't happen… well, I don't think so, my friend, I'll hand it over when the wedding takes place for good…

MERCADET: But without a thousand damned crowns, it won't take place. What! you, who I've seen spend that much out of vanity, on a passing love affair, won't put it to a virtuous action!

VERDELIN: These days there are few virtuous actions… or transactions…

MERCADET: Ha ha! …So clever…you laugh…it must be a reaction!

VERDELIN: Ha ha ha!… *(He drops his hat.)*

MERCADET: *(Picks up the hat and brushes it with his sleeve)* Come now, old man, two friends who knocked about in life! who began together! …The things we said, the things we did! …Eh! Don't you recall the good old days when we swore to be blood brothers?

VERDELIN: Do you recall our party at Rambouillet, when I fought a guards officer on your account?

MERCADET: I gave up Clarisse to you! Ah! We were jolly dogs, we were young! And today we have daughters, daughters old enough to marry! ...If Clarisse were alive, she would scold you for your hesitation!...

VERDELIN: If she had lived, I would never have married!..

MERCADET: Because you know what love is! ...So I may count on you and you'll give me your word of honor that you'll send me—

VERDELIN: The dinner service?

MERCADET: And the thousand crowns...

VERDELIN: Still harping on that? ...I said I can't do it...

MERCADET: *(Aside)* This man will definitely not die of heart trouble... *(Aloud)* So I'm murdered by my best friend!...'Twas ever thus!.. Unmoved by the memory of Clarisse and the despair of a father!... *(He shouts.)* I am in despair, I am going to blow my brains out...

*(*MME MERCADET *and* JULIE *enter.)*

MME MERCADET: What wrong, my dear?

JULIE: Father, you're scaring me with this shouting!

MME MERCADET: Verdelin is here, so you can't be in danger...

JULIE: Good afternoon, sir. What's the matter between you and my father?

MERCADET: Note it well, Verdelin, they run in like two guardian angels protecting their saint the minute they hear my voice! *(Aside)* They heard me! *(To his wife and daughter, taking them by the hands)* Ah, you melt my heart! Verdelin, do you want to destroy a whole family? This proof of their affection gives me courage to fall at your feet. *(He prepares to do so.)*

JULIE: Oh, sir!

*(*JULIE *stops* MERCADET.*)*

JULIE: Let me plead with you for his sake. If it's a matter of money and I'm sure it is, I offer you the guarantee that I will work for it. Oblige my father one more time, he must be in the most terrible anguish to implore you in this way…

MERCADET: *(Aside)* Dear child! *(Aside)* What intonations!.. I wish I could do it that naturally!

MME MERCADET: Monsieur Verdelin, do us this favor, we'll be so grateful, I'll put up the property remaining to me.

VERDELIN: *(To* JULIE*)* Do you know what he's asking?

JULIE: No.

VERDELIN: A thousand crowns to enable you to get married.

JULIE: Ah! Sir, forget what I just said. I do not wish a marriage purchased by my father's humiliation…

MERCADET: *(Aside)* She's magnificent…

VERDELIN: I will go and get the money. *(Exits)*

MERCADET: He's gone for it…

JULIE: Father, why didn't you tell me?

MERCADET: *(Kisses her)* You've saved us! Ah, when shall I be so rich and powerful that I can make him rue the day he did me this favor?..

MME MERCADET: But he's going to bring you the money you asked for…

MERCADET: He sold it to me at too high a price! …He has no idea how to do a favor. Oh! if I could do one, I'd do it with such grace! *(He mimes handing out money.)* Some types of ingratitude call out for vengeance. Ah, my puny Verdelin, you begrudge a loan of a thousand crowns, I have no scruples about doing you out of a hundred thousand!..

MME MERCADET: Don't be unfair, Verdelin gave in.

MERCADET: To Julie's pleas, not mine. Ah, my dear! He got more than a thousand crown's worth of humiliation.

(VERDELIN *returns.)*

VERDELIN: I had the money in my carriage to pay Brédif, but he's away. Here it is, three bags full.

(JUSTIN *brings in the three money-bags and exits.)*

MERCADET: Ah!

MME MERCADET: Sir, you have every right to a mother's gratitude.

VERDELIN: I am lending this money solely to you and your daughter, tomorrow both of you will be good enough to sign the receipt Mercadet will draw up.

JULIE: Sign my ruin!...

MME MERCADET: Be quiet, Julie.

MERCADET: *(Writing)* My dear Verdelin, that's the man I know! Should we put down the interest rate?

VERDELIN: No, no, let's forget the interest...I want to do you a favor and not make a deal...

MERCADET: Daughter, here's your second father!..

(JUSTIN *enters.)*

JUSTIN: Monsieur Minard is asking to see you. *(Exits)*

THÉRÈSE: *(Enters)* Madame, the tradesmen have brought everything...

MME MERCADET: *(Hands the receipt to* VERDELIN*)* I'll be right there.

MERCADET: *(To* VERDELIN*)* You see, you were just in time!

VERDELIN: I shall leave you...

*(*MME MERCADET *and* THÉRÈSE *exit.* MERCADET *sees out* VERDELIN, *and makes a sign to* MINARD *to come in.)*

JULIE: *(To* MINARD) Adolphe, if you want our love to shine as brightly in everyone's eyes, in society parties as in our hearts, be as brave as I have been so far.

MINARD: What's happened?

JULIE: Some rich young man is in the picture, and my father is showing us no mercy…

MINARD: I shall win him over!

MERCADET: *(Re-enters)* Sir, are you in love with my daughter?

MINARD, Yes, sir.

MERCADET: At least, she believes it! You've had the talent to convince her.

MINARD: Your words express a doubt which I would find insulting in anyone else. Why shouldn't I love Mam'selle? I was abandoned by my parents and had no other protection than that of good Monsieur Duval who has been a father to me since I was nine. Your daughter, sir, is the only person who acquainted me with the happiness that comes from being loved. Mam'selle Julie is both my sister and my friend, she is my whole family! …She alone smiled on me, so I love her beyond any ability to express it.

JULIE: Should I stay, father?…

MERCADET: *(To his daughter)* Lap it up! *(To* MINARD*)* Sir, when it comes to young love, I have those down-to-earth ideas which put old men in the doghouse. My mistrust is all the more warrantable because I am not one of those fathers blinded by being a father. I see Julie as she is. Without being ugly, she has none of that beauty that makes people go "Ah!" She is so-so.

MINARD: You are mistaken, sir, I daresay you do not know your Julie..

MERCADET: Indeed I do…just as if…

MINARD: No, sir, you know the Julie everyone sees and knows, but love has transfigured her! Affection, devotion have lent her a ravishing beauty that I alone have created…

JULIE: Father, I'm embarrassed…

MERCADET: You mean, overjoyed… And if he were to repeat such things to you…

MINARD: A hundred times, a thousand times, never enough! …There is no crime in saying them in a father's presence!

MERCADET: You flatter me, I thought I was her father, but you are the father of a Julie I'd like to meet. Come, come, young man, open your eyes! The essential, beautiful qualities of her soul may, I admit, alter the expression on her face, but the complexion? Julie is meek and modest, she knows she has a muddy complexion and her features are a bit…chancy.

JULIE: Father!…

MINARD: You've never been in love then?

MERCADET: Many times! like all men, I've dragged about that golden ball and chain.

MINARD: Ages ago! Nowadays we love in a new improved way…

MERCADET: Just what do you do?

MINARD: We cling to the soul, the ideal.

MERCADET: And that's what makes my daughter pretty? …So, if a woman is broad in the hips, the ideal reduces them! the soul slenderizes her fingers! The ideal makes her eyes sparkling and her feet dainty! the soul clears up her complexion!

MINARD: Certainly.

MERCADET: Those of us who came of age under Napoleon call that…

MINARD: Love!! …Love, pure and holy love!..

MERCADET: Being blindfolded.

JULIE: Father, don't tease two children.

MERCADET: Who are so grown up…

JULIE: Who love one another the way one loves at our age, with a true, pure, lasting passion, because it is based on knowledge of character, on the certainty of a shared enthusiasm for braving life's hardships. In short, two children who love you very much.

MINARD: *(To* MERCADET*)* What an angel!..

MERCADET: *(Aside)* I'll give you angel! *(To his daughter)* Be quiet, daughter. *(To* MINARD*)* So, sir, you adore Julie. She is charming, she has a soul, a mind, a heart. In short, she's your idea of beauty, the perfection you dream of…

MINARD: Ah! then you understand me…

MERCADET: An angel who nevertheless has a touch of the earthbound.

MINARD: To make me happy!..

MERCADET: You love her without any ulterior motive?

MINARD: None.

JULIE: What did I tell you?

MERCADET: *(He takes them by the hands and draws them to him)* Happy children! So you love one another? …What a beautiful romance!… *(To* MINARD*)* You want her for your wife?

MINARD: Yes, sir.

MERCADET: In the face of all obstacles?

MINARD: I am here to overcome them.

MERCADET: Nothing will discourage you?

MINARD: Nothing.

JULIE: Didn't I tell you he loves me!

MERCADET: So it seems! Where could you find a lovelier sight? There is nothing sweeter for a father than to see his daughter loved as she deserves, to see her happy…

JULIE: Won't you give me credit, father, for choosing a son full of lofty sentiments, endowed with a manly soul and…

MINARD: Mam'selle…

JULIE: Yes, sir, yes, I'll have my say too!

MERCADET: Daughter, go to your mother. Leave me to discuss more down-to-earth matters. Whatever the power of the ideal has over female beauty, it has, unfortunately, no influence on income…

*(Exit* JULIE.*)*

MERCADET: We are alone, we can talk turkey. Sir, you do not love my daughter!

MINARD: Why not say, sir, that you have a rich match in mind for Mam'selle Mercadet, that you don't care a whit for her preferences. I would understand, but know that I came to ask for her hand only after I had won her heart.

MERCADET: Her heart? You wretch! What do you mean?

MINARD: I love Mam'selle Julie honorably.

MERCADET: Very well! Luckily it's just idealism! But you owe me the whole truth now that we've come this far… You've written to one another?

MINARD: Yes, sir, letters full of love.

MERCADET: *(Aside)* Ah, poor girl! she's been reading love letters! With that face! It's her head not her heart that will suffer!… *(Aloud)* Sir, angels have a thousand perfections, but they do not have an income invested in government bonds, and Julie…

MINARD: Ah, sir! I am ready for any sacrifice, all I want is Julie.

MERCADET: You've said that no obstacle will daunt you.

MINARD: None.

MERCADET: Well, I'm going to share a secret on which depend the honor and peace of the family you insist on entering.

MINARD: *(Aside)* What is he going to say?

MERCADET: I am stony broke, sir, a ruined man. If you want Julie, you're welcome to her, she'll be much better off with you, poor as you are, than in her father's house… Not only has she no dowry, but she is lumbered with destitute parents… worse than destitute…

MINARD: Worse than destitute…there's nothing worse than that!

MERCADET: There is, sir, for we have debts, heaps of debts, clamoring to be paid…

MINARD: *(Aside)* A trick out of a comedy. He's testing me. *(Aloud)* Well, sir, I am young, my future lies ahead of me, I don't lack energy or ambition. Today no one will come from afar to ask me anything other than my name. I will succeed...I will enjoy the happiness of making the woman I love rich.

MERCADET: Sounds familiar. I ruined myself for Madame Mercadet, so I could keep her in the luxurious way of life to which she was accustomed. In my day I too sacrificed to an ideal, but creditors don't care about poetic ideas, imagination, happiness!

MINARD: *(Aside)* He's jeering at me, he's rich.

MERCADET: So my secret doesn't scare you away?

MINARD: No, sir. No thought of self-interest besmirches my love.

MERCADET: Well said, young man. Oh, you spoke that line marvelously. *(Aside)* Stubborn as a mule. *(Aloud)* So you love my daughter enough to pay a high price for the happiness of marrying her?

MINARD: What more can I give than my life?

MERCADET: A love so sincere must be rewarded.

MINARD: At last!..

MERCADET: I can have complete confidence in you?

MINARD: I deserve it, sir.

MERCADET: Wait! *(He exits.)*

MINARD: *(Once he's alone)* In my place, lots of young men faced with this situation would have trembled, weakened! When a father that rich has a daughter who isn't beautiful (for Julie is plain, no more), he's got good reason to find out if she's being wooed exclusively for her fortune... Oh, for a timid fellow, I've been fantastic! He's got good sense, that father. Of course Julie does love me, I'm the only man who ever spoke to her of love, and my eloquence even persuaded me. But I'll make her happy, I'll love her the way a man should love his wife. Yes, I do love her. Perhaps, by dint of studying someone, you end up understanding her, and then you see her soul beyond the veil of flesh. Julie has a beautiful soul. After all, it's a woman's qualities and not her beauty that make happy marriages! Besides, people marry even the ugliest women. And then! a woman who loves us knows how to make herself attractive!..

MERCADET: *(Returns)* Here, son-in-law, are the family papers which will testify to our fortune…

MINARD: Sir…

MERCADET: Or lack thereof…read them. Here's a copy of the writ of attachment on our furniture! I paid a good deal to the landlord for the right to keep it here. This morning he wanted to sell it all. Here you'll find summonses by the score, and alas! a judicial arrest warrant from yesterday… you see things are getting serious… Have a look at all the protests for non-payment, all the judgments, all my files arranged in order. For, young man, bear this in mind: when your affairs are in disorder, order is paramount. When disorder is well organized it can be dealt with and controlled! What can a creditor say when he sees his debt's been given a number! I took the government as my model, everything in alphabetical order. I have not yet made inroads on the letter A.

MINARD: You haven't paid anything?

MERCADET: Not much. But am I not open and above board?

MINARD: Wide open!…

MERCADET: So now you know the state of my finances, you understand book-keeping… Look! The total: three hundred and eighty thousand…

MINARD: Yes, sir, the total amount is on the books.

MERCADET: You've read it… You can't complain? A father eager to unload his daughter would have tried to deceive you, he would have promised a fictitious dowry, a profitable income! People play those kinds of tricks! ...More often than you'd think! Lots of fathers take advantage of a love like yours to exploit it! But here you're dealing with an honorable man... One can be in debt and still be a man of honor... You make me tremble when you work your own undoing to my daughter's face with your fine protestations. Marrying a poor girl when you've no more salary than two thousand francs is like marrying a protested I O U with a writ of execution.

MINARD: You think so, sir! So I would be making your daughter miserable!

MERCADET: Ah, young man! Now my daughter Julie wears her true complexion..

MINARD: Yes, sir.

MERCADET: Shake hands! You've won my respect. You're a likely lad, you lie so neatly!...

MINARD: Monsieur Mercadet!

MERCADET: You could be a cabinet minister, the senate would believe every word...

MINARD: Sir!

MERCADET: What, are you going to quarrel with me? I'm the one to complain, young man! You've upset the peace of my family, you've put outlandish ideas about love in my daughter's head, ideas that may make it hard for her to be happy once she's concocted an ideal for herself...a ridiculous ideal. Julie is several months older than you, your counterfeit love for her offers her allurements no girl in her position can resist...

MINARD: Sir, if our mutual poverty separates us, I at least am without reproach! I love Mam'selle Julie! A poor disinherited fellow like myself, can he find anyone better?

MERCADET: Fancy phrases! ...You have done the damage. Now you have to repair it.

MINARD: Believe me, sir...

MERCADET: Not another word... Proofs... You shall return the letters my daughter wrote to you.

MINARD: This very day...

MERCADET: And you will help an unhappy father get her married. If you love Julie, force yourself to assist me. She has to have a fortune and a name. You can pretend to be smitten with her, there's nothing dishonorable in playing the role of a self-sacrificing lover. In France everyone immediately wants what everyone else desires. A young lady courted, fought over, acquires ideal attractions. Yes, if our happiness makes somebody else mad with envy, we're all the happier. Envy lurks at the bottom of the human heart like a viper in its den. Ah! you catch my drift... As for Julie *(He calls* JULIE.*)*, I leave it to you to effect the change. She wouldn't believe me if I told her you were throwing her over...

MINARD: How can I do it after all I've said and written to her?

*(*MERCADET *exits.)*

MINARD: I'd rather be a hundred feet underground. Marry her? I have a salary of eighteen hundred francs, not enough for one person to live on, what would become of the two of us? There she is... she doesn't seem to be the same even now! I have to get used to seeing her through three hundred thousand francs dowry! ...Here we go...

*(Enter* JULIE.*)*

JULIE: Well, Adolphe?

MINARD: Mam'selle!...

JULIE: Mam'selle? I'm not Julie anymore? You've settled things with my father?

MINARD: Yes…I mean…

JULIE: Oh, money has already poked a hole in love. But I hope you've won over my father…

MINARD: Ah, Julie, your father has reasons that are judicial…sorry…judicious.

JULIE: What went on between the two of you? Adolphe, have you stopped loving me?

MINARD: I still do!…

JULIE: I've had misgivings …

MINARD: A great change has occurred in our situation.

JULIE: You haven't overcome all obstacles?

MINARD: Your father hasn't told you of his situation, it's ghastly, Julie, because it means poverty for you. There are some men who face poverty energetically. You don't know what I'm like, I'm one of those men poverty lays low… Listen! …I couldn't stand the sight of your unhappiness.

JULIE: I would have the courage for both of us. You'd never see me without a smile on my face. And besides, I would never be a burden. My china painting would earn almost as much as your job; and, without being rich, I promise you comfort will reign in our pretty home.

MINARD: *(Aside)* No one can love the way a poor girl can…

JULIE: What are you saying, sir?

MINARD: I've never seen you so lovely!.. *(Aside)* Love is driving me crazy! …I have to put an end to this. *(Aloud)* But…

JULIE: "But", Adolphe, is a weasel word…

MINARD: Your father has appealed to my finer feelings. He proved to me how selfish a passion love is.

JULIE: Not when it's two.

MINARD: Even when it's three! He showed me the difference in your fate if you were rich. Julie, there are two ways of loving…

JULIE: There's only one.

MINARD: The love that dooms you to poverty is senseless, the love that sacrifices itself to your happiness is heroic!

JULIE: My only happiness, Adolphe, is to be yours!

MINARD: Ah! if you'd heard your father, he asked me to give you up!

JULIE: And you have?..

MINARD: I'm trying, I wish I could but I can't. Something within me keeps repeating I will never be loved more than I am by you…

JULIE: Oh! of course, sir, my love! …Oh, why do I go on talking about it?

MINARD: I can accept it only by sacrificing myself…

JULIE: Goodbye, goodbye, sir!

*(Exit* MINARD.*)*

JULIE: He's going, he'll never come back! Oh, God in heaven!… *(She looks at herself in a mirror.)* Beauty, peerless asset, the only one that can't be bought though it is only a mirage, a promise, well, I don't have you! Oh! I know, I've tried to replace you with affection, kindness, meekness, absolute devotion which forces one to deposit one's life like a grain of incense on an altar… And now all the hopes of a poor ugly girl have flown out the window. My cherished idol has just shattered into smithereens before my eyes! …

That phrase: "I'm beautiful, I can charm, fulfill my destiny as a woman, provide happiness, receive it!," that intoxicating idea will never occur to console my heart! …No more illusions, I've been dreaming… *(She wipes away a few tears.)* I'll let my tears flow and not wipe them away. I am alone in life. He didn't love me! I lent my own qualities, my own feelings to dress up a phantom that has vanished into thin air! …and my grief will look so ridiculous that I must hide it in my innermost being… Come, one last sigh for my first love and then let's settle down to becoming, as so many women are, the plaything of random events in an unknown life! To save my father, let's be Madame de la Brive. Let's set aside the glittering crown of a love that is unique, virtuous and shared!…

END OF ACT TWO

# ACT THREE

MINARD: *(Alone)* If I only were the department head of a government office, I would never return these letters! Before handing them over, I've reread them. They express a beautiful soul, infinite affection. Oh, poverty! …it may have swallowed up as many great loves as great geniuses! What respect we should pay the heroes who have subdued it, they are heroes twice over!

*(*JULIE *enters.)*

JULIE: I saw you come in and so here I am! Oh, I have no pride…

MINARD: And I no strength.

JULIE: You don't love me as much as I love you, you're a man! If only you felt a single regret, Adolphe?…

MINARD: What then?

JULIE: I would call off this marriage without my father knowing why.

MINARD: After that?

JULIE: We would have the future ahead of us! And the two of us would know how to get rich…

MINARD: The chances for our future are zero. Listen to me, Julie! After I left you, I felt so guilty that I deserve to be forgiven. Think me greedy or ambitious, at least I'll be sincere. I thought your fortune would provide the leverage for the efforts I dreamt of making for you!

I'm alone in the world, it was natural to expect help from the woman I wanted to make my companion. Perhaps I even counted on the pleasure you would take in my attentions and be attracted to me, I was so much in need of support. But when I came to know you, I felt a genuine affection for you, and what your father told me has not extinguished it…

JULIE: Truly!

MINARD: Yes, Julie, I feel I love you, and if you have as much faith in me as I have love for you, together we can brave life's hardships!..

JULIE: Enough! Enough! That confession will do. It cost me dear to learn you had selfish motives… Not another word. I am happy.

MINARD: Truly, Julie, I would be able to suffer a great deal, but you? Are you proof against misfortune? At first we will have nothing to share but afflictions…

JULIE: I forgive your ambition, your ulterior motives. Forgive my persistence. Since you love me, anything seems possible…

MINARD: Then, I stand for doubt and you stand for hope.

JULIE: I shall try to stay uncommitted for a while longer. There is a voice in my heart that keeps saying we will be happy.

MINARD: I recently received a letter from my mother who writes, she abandoned me only for my own good and predicts better days ahead! Perhaps my fate will change.

MME MERCADET: *(Enters)* Julie, your father will be angry if he sees you engaged in conversation, especially with this gentleman, instead of getting dressed. Monsieur de Méricourt and Monsieur de la Brive might come upon you in this everyday outfit.

MINARD: Madam, this visit is not an intrusion. I came to return my letters to Mam'selle and request the return of mine, as Monsieur Mercadet wished.

JULIE: Mother, now you know we love one another. Won't you shield your daughter from unhappiness?

MME MERCADET: Julie, your father, in his situation, needs a son-in-law who will be useful to him and assist him in his negotiations. If the marriage falls through, he is lost.

JULIE: And my life is over.

MINARD: Monsieur Duval, ex-cashier of Monsieur Mercadet and Monsieur Godeau…

MME MERCADET: Is also one of Monsieur Mercadet's creditors.

MINARD: Yes, madam, but I just spoke to him about Monsieur Mercadet's problems. *(Mme Mercadet flinches.)* Oh, he's already familiar with them, madam, and yet he doesn't think them insuperable. He's willing to take charge of the liquidation.

MME MERCADET: My husband, go into liquidation! You don't know him! Like the gambler crouched over the fatal card-table, he still hopes to come up trumps. I don't know what he's capable of to preserve the right to make a fortune. Besides, you see he's about to marry off his daughter!.. Go into liquidation, him! Give up business, why, it's his life! …Sir, I let you into this secret to explain how little chance there is of making him go back on his decision. How can I as a wife and mother blame Monsieur Mercadet for choosing a rich match for his daughter when I see myself on the verge of utter poverty? …Monsieur de la Brive has a name, family connections.

JULIE: *(To her mother)* Stop, mother! …Think of Adolphe's situation!

JUSTIN: *(Enters)* Monsieur de la Brive and Monsieur de Mèricourt.

JULIE: *(To* MINARD*)* Come along, sir! I'll give you back your letters.

MME MERCADET: *(To* JUSTIN*)* Ask them to wait here, I'll send the master to receive them. Come, let's change our clothes, Julie.

*(The women and* MINARD *exit.* MÉRICOURT *and* DE LA BRIVE enter.)

JUSTIN: The ladies are still dressing and ask the gentlemen to wait a moment. The master will be here shortly. *(Exits)*

MÉRICOURT: Well, my dear fellow, you've finally sailed into a safe port, soon to be officially engaged to Mam'selle Mercadet. Steer your boat cautiously, the father's a shark!

DE LA BRIVE: That's what worries me! He'll be a hard nut to crack.

MÉRICOURT: I'm not so sure. Mercadet is a speculator, rich today, possibly broke tomorrow. From the little his wife told me about his affairs, I think he's overjoyed to put part of his fortune in his daughter's name and get a son-in-law to assist him in his schemes.

DE LA BRIVE: There's an idea! It suits me, but suppose he asks too many questions?

MÉRICOURT: I've given Madame Mercadet a glowing account of you! A woman of forty, my dear fellow, believes whatever she's told by anyone who lavishes attentions on her…

DE LA BRIVE: This is too good to be true…

MÉRICOURT: Are you going to lose your dandy's poise? I realize your position is a tricky one. I imagine you'd have to be at your lowest ebb before you'd get married.

Marriage is suicide for dandies, after such a glorious career. *(He lowers his voice.)* Tell me—can you hold out much longer?

DE LA BRIVE: If I didn't use my original name Michonnin for the process servers and de la Brive in high society, I'd already be banished from the boulevard. Women and I, as you know, are mutually destructive; and given the current moral climate, to meet with an Englishwoman, an amiable dowager, an amorous El Dorado, they're an extinct species, like the dinosaurs!

MÉRICOURT: Gambling?

DE LA BRIVE: Oh! Gambling is a safe expedient only for certain confidence tricksters, and I'm not fool enough to risk dishonor for a few short-term gains. Publicity, my dear fellow, has ruined all the careers by which people used to make fortunes. So, for a hundred thousand francs in I O Us, the money lenders will give me only ten thousand in silver. Pierquin sent me to a mini-Pierquin, old man Violette, who told my broker it would cost too much just for the official stamps… My tailor refuses to see I have a future…my horse is living on credit. As to that well-dressed little wretch, my groom, I don't know how he breathes or where he feeds. I don't dare peer into that mystery. Now, since our civilization is not as advanced as that of the Jews who cancel all debts every half-century, one has to pay with one's person. What they're saying about me is appalling… A young man very well-thought-of in the fashionable world, reasonably lucky at cards, with passable features, not yet twenty-eight, to marry the daughter of a rich speculator…she's ugly, you say?

MÉRICOURT: Oh well!..

DE LA BRIVE: That's a bit much! But I'm getting tired of an idle life… Of course I realized that the shortest way to make money is to work... But...our misfortune, we lot, we aristocrats, is we're ready for everything but not particularly good at anything! A man like me, capable of inspiring passions and living up to them, can't be a clerk or a soldier. Society has provided no career for men like us! Very well, I'll go into business with Mercadet. He's one of the greatest of the wheeler-dealers. Together we'll rattle the business world. Are you sure he won't allocate his daughter less than a hundred and fifty thousand francs?

MÉRICOURT: My dear fellow, judging by Madame Mercadet's wardrobe...anyway...you see her at all the first nights, the play, the opera. She's the last word in elegance!...

DE LA BRIVE: I'm rather elegant myself, and I don't own a thing...

MÉRICOURT: True, but look around...it all reeks of ostentation! Oh! they are very well off!

DE LA BRIVE: The bourgeois idea of splendor...cosy, promising...

MÉRICOURT: Besides, the mother has firm principles! At forty she has scruples! For eighteen months, I've seen nothing in her conduct which isn't very...respectable. Do you have enough time to pull it off?

DE LA BRIVE: I'm up to scratch. At the club yesterday I won enough to do nicely on the groom's present of a tenth of the dowry. I'll pay a little down, and owe the rest.

MÉRICOURT: Minus what you owe me, what do your debts come to?

DE LA BRIVE: A mere trifle! A hundred and fifty thousand francs, which my father-in-law will reduce to fifty thousand! I'll have a hundred thousand francs left to launch my first business deal. I always said I'd never get rich till I hadn't a penny left.

MÉRICOURT: Mercadet is crafty, he'll interrogate you about your fortune. Are you prepared?

DE LA BRIVE: I own the La Brive estate, three thousand acres in Les Landes, worth thirty thousand francs, mortgaged for forty-five thousand and capable of being floated by a joint-stock company to excavate something or other with capital of a hundred thousand crowns… You can't imagine how much this property has already made me!

MÉRICOURT: Your name, your horse and your lands do double duty.

DE LA BRIVE: Not so loud!..

MÉRICOURT: So you've made up your mind?

DE LA BRIVE: Especially since I'm going into politics…

MÉRICOURT: You're slippery enough for it.

DE LA BRIVE: I'll start by being a journalist.

MÉRICOURT: But you've never written two lines in your life!

DE LA BRIVE: Some journalists write and some don't. The former are the editors, the workhorses who pull the cart. The others, the owners, are the enterpreneurs. They feed them a bit of oats and keep the capital. I'll be an owner. You sink your chin into your collar and say: "The Eastern question is one of great importance, surpassing influence, about which there can be only one opinion." You sum up a debate by declaiming: "England, sir, will always get the better of us!" or else you reply to a long-winded speech you weren't listening to: "We are heading for an abyss. We have not yet evolved all the evolutions of the revolutionary phase!" To a cabinet minister: "Sir, I think something needs to be done on this issue." You weigh your words, run to and fro, make yourself useful, take steps a man in power can't take himself… You're reputed to come up with the themes of articles that attract attention! …Then you publish a yellow-back tome on some Utopia so well written, so powerful that no one opens it and everyone claims he's read it! And so you become a person of consequence and eventually a somebody instead of a something!

MÉRICOURT: Dear me, your description is only too true nowadays.

DE LA BRIVE: We see startling proofs of it! To share in political power, these days they don't ask what good you can do, but what harm! You must not only be competent, you must inspire fear! Everyone in politics is a nervous wreck, because of all those piles of dirty linen in every closet that no one can get clean…I know our era inside out. While I dine, play cards, get in debt, I learn my lessons in political science. I study those little closets. So the day after my wedding I shall adopt an earnest, profound air and principles! I have a choice. Here in France we've got a list of principles as varied as a restaurant menu. I shall be a socialist. I like the sound of it. In every era, my dear fellow, there are adjectives that are the password to ambition! Before the Revolution, the word was economist. After the defeat of Napoleon, liberal. Tomorrow's party will call itself social, perhaps because it's anti-social, for, in France, you must always examine the opposite of a word to find its true meaning.

MÉRICOURT: You're investing your frivolous hobbies at very high interest.

DE LA BRIVE: You said it.

MÉRICOURT: But, between you and me, this is masquerade jargon that passes for wit among those who don't speak it. What will you do if you need to know something?

DE LA BRIVE: My friend, in every field, business, science, art or literature, a man needs grounding, specialized knowledge or special gifts to prove his ability. But in politics, my dear fellow, a man achieves everything and becomes everything by means of a few words..

MÉRICOURT: Which are?

DE LA BRIVE: "The principles of my friends…the party to which I belong…" You'll see!

*(Enter* MINARD. *They bow to each other.)*

MINARD: The gentleman is no doubt Monsieur de la Brive?

DE LA BRIVE: Yes, sir.

MÉRICOURT: This is the little fellow the chamber-maid mentioned who's courting the heiress.

DE LA BRIVE: Or the inheritance…

MÉRICOURT: And was turned down for you…

*(*DE LA BRIVE *stares at* MINARD *through his lorgnette.)*

MINARD: You are lucky, sir, you have the privileges of wealth. You take a fancy to a young lady, you marry her…

DE LA BRIVE: Allow me to believe, sir, that even without a fortune, I would have personal advantages…

MINARD: Ah, if I had your fortune!..

MÉRICOURT: *(To* DE LA BRIVE*)* Poor fellow! There'd be slim pickings.

MINARD: I would never give up this treasure of grace and perfection to anyone, but a father's authority is on your side.

DE LA BRIVE: And you, sir?

MINARD: I have only my love for Julie.

(MERCADET *enters and listens for a moment.)*

DE LA BRIVE: Sir, I do not see how I can be either useful or accommodating to you.

MINARD: Sir, since chance has thrown us together, I feel firm enough to say: Make her rich and happy.

MERCADET: *(Aside)* What's he saying? Make her rich? He might compromise everything! *(He shows himself.)*

DE LA BRIVE: *(To* MÉRICOURT*)* He's amusing, this little young man. He should be encouraged to stick around, for if my bride is very ugly!..

MERCADET: Good afternoon, my dear Méricourt, have you seen my wife? *(To* DE LA BRIVE*)* The ladies are making you wait! Ah, primping and preening! *(He looks at* MINARD.*)* Monsieur Minard, I thought you a man of good taste and we've made things abundantly clear.

MINARD: Sorry, sir.

MERCADET: Passion may justify many things, but there are certain niceties which must never be ignored…

MINARD: I understand, sir.

MÉRICOURT: *(To* MERCADET*)* He's not so dangerous!

MERCADET: *(Undertone to* MINARD*)* You should act more heart-broken. *(Aloud)* And so, goodbye, my dear fellow! *(Undertone)* At least breathe a sigh!

MINARD: *(To the young men)* Goodbye, gentlemen! *(To* MERCADET*)* Be indulgent, sir, to a man who has lost his happiness!

(MERCADET *escorts him out.)*

MERCADET: Poor young man! I may have been severe but I do feel for him, he adores my daughter! What could I do? He has only ten thousand francs a year and a job…

DE LA BRIVE: That wouldn't go very far!

MERCADET: You'd vegetate! Ah! He figured out what Julie is worth, and since he's socially adept, he got my wife on his side. But he has the defect of being an orphan with a living father and mother whom he cares for more than they care for him. Given that situation, I can't imagine how he could make a play for the daughter of a man who knows his way around.

DE LA BRIVE: You're not the man to give your rich and intelligent daughter's hand to just anybody.

MERCADET: Certainly not. But, sir, meanwhile, before the ladies come in, let's talk serious business.

DE LA BRIVE: *(To* MÉRICOURT*)* Here comes the hard part!

MERCADET: Do you love my daughter?

DE LA BRIVE: Passionately!

MERCADET: *(Aside)* That's a bad beginning. *(Aloud)* Passionately? That's too strong for a happy household.

MÉRICOURT: *(To* DE LA BRIVE*)* Don't overdo it. *(To* MERCADET*)* My friend adores music and Mam'selle Julie's voice enraptured him.

MERCADET: The gentleman has heard my daughter sing? Where was that?

DE LA BRIVE: At a banker's, an ex-something…

MERCADET: Ah! Verdelin!…

DE LA BRIVE: Verdelin.

MÉRICOURT: Yes, Verdelin.

DE LA BRIVE: She has so much soul, Mam'selle Julie!..

MERCADET: Oh, the soul and the ideal are the be-all and end-all. I'm a man of my time. I can understand it,

I can! The ideal, life's perfection! Sir, it's a result of the law of contrasts. However crass I may be when doing business, I feel the pull of the ideal in my sentiments. So, I haunt the Stock Exchange while my daughter soars through the clouds... She is so poetic! ...Oh! she is all soul! ...I see you admire the Lake school of poetry...

DE LA BRIVE: No, sir...

MERCADET: How can you love Julie if you don't cultivate the ideal?

MÉRICOURT: *(To* DE LA BRIVE*)* Give him an explanation.

DE LA BRIVE: *(To* MÉRICOURT*)* Wait! *(To* MERCADET*)* Sir, I am ambitious.

MERCADET: That's better.

DE LA BRIVE: In Mam'selle Julie I saw a delicate creature endowed with a fine mind and charming manners, who would never be out of place in whatever post fortune were to elevate me. That's an essential requirement for a politician.

MERCADET: I understand! You can always find a wife, but it's very rare for a man who wants to be a cabinet minister or an ambassador to turn up (let's be blunt, we're all men here!) a mate! ...You are a clever fellow, sir.

DE LA BRIVE: Sir, I am a socialist!

MERCADET: What new venture's that? ...But now let's discuss money matters.

MÉRICOURT: I think our notaries might deal with it.

DE LA BRIVE: Monsieur Mercadet is right. It concerns us personally!

MERCADET: The gentleman's right too.

DE LA BRIVE: Sir, my entire fortune consists of the estate of La Brive. It has been in my family for a hundred and fifty years, and I hope will never pass from us.

MERCADET: Nowadays you're better off with capital. You can lay your hands on capital. If a revolution breaks out, and we've seen plenty of those, capital follows us wherever we go. Land, on the other hand, land has to shell out for everyone. It stands still like a dummy attracting taxation, while capital takes it on the lam! ...But that is no real obstacle. How extensive is it?

DE LA BRIVE: Three thousand acres, undivided.

MERCADET: Undivided?

MÉRICOURT: Didn't I tell you!

MERCADET: Sir!

DE LA BRIVE: A château—

MERCADET: Sir...

DE LA BRIVE: And salt marshes, which can be exploited as soon as the local authorities issue a permit and could then yield enormous returns!

MERCADET: Sir, where have you been all my life? ... Your land, then, must be near the sea?

DE LA BRIVE: About two miles from it.

MERCADET: And it is located?

DE LA BRIVE: Close to Bordeaux.

MERCADET: You have vineyards?

DE LA BRIVE: No, sir, fortunately not, because it's a great nuisance finding buyers for wine. Besides, vineyards cost a lot to keep up... No, my land doesn't demand much in the way of expense... It was planted with pine trees by my grandfather, a genius clever enough to make sacrifices for his children... Ah! I also have personal property you're familiar with...

MERCADET: Just a moment, sir! …A businessman must dot all his i's.

DE LA BRIVE: *(To* MÉRICOURT*)* Uh-oh!

MERCADET: Your estate, your marshland, I see the profit that can be made out of those marshes! You can form a joint-stock company for the exploitation of the La Brive salt marshes! There's over a million in it, sir.

DE LA BRIVE: I'm well aware of that, sir. All that's needed is a stock offering.

MERCADET: *(Aside)* That remark suggests a degree of intelligence. *(Aloud)* Have you any debts? Is your estate mortgaged? Because we can own land officially even though the property secretly belongs to our creditors.

MÉRICOURT: You wouldn't think much of my friend if he didn't have any debts!.

DE LA BRIVE: I will be frank, sir. There is a mortgage of forty-five thousand francs on the La Brive estate…

MERCADET: *(Aside)* Naïve young man! *(Aloud)* You could… *(He takes him by the hands.)* You have my consent, you shall be my son-in-law, the husband I have chosen! You have no idea how lucky you are!

DE LA BRIVE: *(To* MÉRICOURT*)* This is too good to be true!

MÉRICOURT: *(To* DE LA BRIVE*)* He's dazzled by the opportunity to speculate.

MERCADET: *(Aside)* With permits, which can be bought, we could create salt-mines. I'm saved! *(Aloud)* Let me shake your hand, English-style. *(He shakes his hand.)* You live up to all my expectations of a son-in-law. I can see you're not one of those short-sighted provincial landowners, we'll see eye to eye.

DE LA BRIVE: You must not take it amiss, sir, if I, for my part, inquire as to—

MERCADET: My daughter's fortune? ...Oh! she marries with her own property; her mother gives up to her holdings (merely real estate), a small farm of only two hundred acres but in the very heart of Brie, with well-built barns. As for me, I shall give her two hundred thousand francs, the interest of which I shall allow her to use until you find a secure investment for it. Young man, I won't deceive you, we're going to go into business. I'm fond of you, I like you. Are you ambitious?

DE LA BRIVE: Indeed, sir.

MERCADET: You love luxury, spending money. You want to shine in Paris...

DE LA BRIVE: Indeed, sir.

MERCADET: Play a leading role there.

DE LA BRIVE: Indeed, sir.

MERCADET: I thought so, from your demeanor. I know men. You have the bearing of those sure that they have a future.

MÉRICOURT: *(Aside)* And who always borrow on it.

MERCADET: Well, now that I'm old and obliged to transfer my ambition to a second self, I shall leave that brilliant role to you.

DE LA BRIVE: Sir, had I been forced to choose from all the fathers-in-law in Paris, I should have picked you. You are a man after my own heart.

MERCADET: Youth is made for pleasure. You and my daughter must shine! Have a townhouse, carriages, throw parties! Julie is a clever girl, she'll play that role marvelously. Look, let's not be like those people who shoot into the sky for a few days and immediately plunge downwards like Parisian rockets... Make your wife's fortune impregnable!

MÉRICOURT: And pregnant.

DE LA BRIVE: Suppose we don't succeed?

MERCADET: Suppose we succeed too well…

DE LA BRIVE: There's always a crust of bread.

MERCADET: Nowadays a crust of bread is three horses in your stable, a multi-story house, the ability to give dinner parties, have a box at the theatre.

DE LA BRIVE: Ah, sir, let me shake your hand, English-style. *(Another hand-shake.)*

MÉRICOURT: *(Aside)* This is going too smoothly…

DE LA BRIVE: *(Aside)* He's diving headfirst into my fishpond.

MERCADET: *(Aside)* He agrees to a limited income…

MÉRICOURT: *(To* DE LA BRIVE*)* Are you satisfied?

DE LA BRIVE: No. I don't see the money to pay off my debts.

MÉRICOURT: Wait. *(To* MERCADET*)* My friend doesn't dare mention it, but he's too honest to hide it. He has a few small debts.

MERCADET: Speak frankly, sir, I understand such things perfectly… Let's see, these pesky nuisances…some fifty thousand francs?

MÉRICOURT: Just about…

DE LA BRIVE: Just about.

MERCADET: A mere trifle.

DE LA BRIVE: *(Laughing)* A mere trifle!

MERCADET: It'll be like a little farce you and your wife will act out. Yes, leave me the pleasure of… Anyway, we will pay them… *(Aside)* in shares of the La Brive salt mines. *(Aloud)* It's such a paltry sum. *(Aside)* We'll up the value of the salt marsh another hundred thousand francs…I'm saved!

DE LA BRIVE: *(To* MÉRICOURT*)* I'm saved!

*(Enter* MME MERCADET *and* JULIE.*)*

MERCADET: Here are my wife and daughter.

MÉRICOURT: Madam, may I introduce Monsieur de la Brive, a young friend of mine, who regards your daughter with admiration…

DE LA BRIVE: Passionate admiration…

MERCADET: *(To* DE LA BRIVE*)* You must think they're Spanish ladies, I see. Eh! What a complexion! A genuine Andalusian, capable of braving the storms of life.

DE LA BRIVE: A blonde would have put me off!

MERCADET: My daughter is just the wife for a politician.

DE LA BRIVE: *(Surveys* JULIE *through his lorgnette)(To* MERCADET*)* Expensively dressed. *(To* MME MERCADET*)* Like mother, like daughter! Madam, I entrust my hopes to your protection.

MME MERCADET: With an introduction from Monsieur Méricourt, the gentleman is more than welcome.

JULIE: *(To her mother)* What a fop!…

MERCADET: *(To his daughter)* Immensely rich! we'll all be millionaires! And an extremely witty fellow. So be pleasant, it's imperative!

JULIE: What do you want me to say to a dandy I've met for the first time and whom you want to make my husband.

DE LA BRIVE: Mam'selle, may I be allowed to hope you don't object to my suit?

JULIE: I am bound to obey my father.

DE LA BRIVE: *(Aside)* Proud the way ugly girls are. You have to put in more effort for them than for duchesses.

JULIE: *(Aside)* He's good-looking, he's rich, why is he interested in me? There's something peculiar about this.

DE LA BRIVE: *(Aside)* Here goes! *(Aloud)* Mam'selle, young ladies are not always aware of the feelings they inspire! For two months now I've aspired to the happiness of paying you my respects.

JULIE: What could be more flattering, sir, than to find I've attracted your attention?

MME MERCADET: *(To* JULIE*)* He's very well-spoken.

JULIE: *(To* MME MERCADET*)* Mother, leave it to me to find out if I can be happy by marrying this gentleman.

MERCADET: *(To* MÉRICOURT*)* You can count on my gratitude, sir. We owe you our happiness, for our daughter's and our own are the same.

MME MERCADET: Monsieur de la Brive and his friend will honor us by accepting our invitation to an informal dinner...

MERCADET: Just pot-luck. *(To* DE LA BRIVE*)* If you'll be so kind?

MME MERCADET: Monsieur de Méricourt, won't you come and see the painting we've just put up in a charity raffle? *(To* JULIE*)* We'll leave you to chat a while with him.

JULIE: Thank you so much, mother!

MME MERCADET: Monsieur Mercadet?

*(*MME MERCADET *exits with* MÉRICOURT.*)*

MERCADET: She's a romantic like all young ladies with heart and imagination. Stroll with her down poetry lane.

DE LA BRIVE: *(To* MERCADET*)* Romanticism is the abc of modern sentiment, I could write reams of it. In short, it's the art of concealing actions with fancy phrases.

MERCADET: *(On his way out)* He really is very clever, that young man.

JULIE: Sir, please don't think it strange that a poor girl like myself requires proof of your affection. My mistrust is driven by my awareness that I am not very attractive…

DE LA BRIVE: Such modesty is in itself an attraction, Mam'selle!…

JULIE: If I had that wondrous beauty that stirs up sudden passions, I might find reasons for your interest; but to love me you have to be familiar with my heart and we are meeting for the first time…

DE LA BRIVE: Mam'selle, there are inexplicable affinities…

JULIE: So you love me without knowing why?

DE LA BRIVE: Explanations make love fly out the window! The finest feelings are the involuntary ones. So, the first time I saw you…

JULIE: Ah, so this isn't the first!

DE LA BRIVE: Why, mam'selle, I've loved you for the last two months! Ever since I heard you at the last concert at Monsieur Verdelin's, and your voice revealed to me… the whole of your soul.

JULIE: What did I sing? Do you remember?..

DE LA BRIVE: *(Aside)* Deuce take it! *(Aloud)* I remember only that the impression was delightful…

JULIE: So you love me? Really and truly?

DE LA BRIVE: Mam'selle, I've known that you are a lady of courage, endowed with rare refinement in both feelings and ideas, highly educated as well; that you would know how to launch a salon in Paris, be the companion of a politician, and, if I may say so, not all women know how to manage a great fortune. Many social climbers have been encumbered by daughters and made the mistake of marrying them off when their careers were just beginning. And, in the ocean of politics, when a woman is not a sturdy tug-boat, she's an embargo! I doubted I would ever come across a woman who could understand and work for my future. I saw you and I said, "I can be an ambassador. The woman I love will be the rival of the corseted diplomat's wives sent us by Russia!"

JULIE: *(Aside)* Men are all so ambitious nowadays!… *(Aloud)* So, you're ambitious and in love? Your affection is lined with self-interest…

DE LA BRIVE: *(Aside)* She's no fool! *(Aloud)* Mam'selle, love is full of so many things!..

JULIE: Yours is full of so many things that it's bound to include devotion…

DE LA BRIVE: Above all!

JULIE: So, my family?

DE LA BRIVE: Becomes my own.

JULIE: Nothing will stop you then?

DE LA BRIVE: Nothing.

JULIE: I love another young man, sir.

DE LA BRIVE: I've seen him, and I confess he made me wonder about your poor judgment. That young man is no match for you at all.

JULIE: You're mistaken, sir, I can give him up only in favor of a great devotion! Well, if you rescue my father from ruin, I will love you…I will forget the love

I thought would be everlasting and I will be the most faithful, loving wife, and I… *(Aside)* Ah! I'm choking…

DE LA BRIVE: *(Aside)* She scares me… she's putting me through test after test, like a Masonic initiation… *(Aloud)* I hope by my love to deserve everything that women usually owe their husbands unconditionally. But stop putting my sincere passion to the test. Mam'selle, your father and I have come to an understanding about money matters.

JULIE: He told you everything?

DE LA BRIVE: Everything!

JULIE: You know he's ruined?

DE LA BRIVE: Ruined!

JULIE: *(Aside)* Ah, I'm saved! *(Aloud)* He owes about three hundred thousand francs.

DE LA BRIVE: He…owes…three…

JULIE: Where's your devotion now?

DE LA BRIVE: *(Aside)* Devotion! It's by marrying her… If she thinks a person can take on a lifetime mate like her free, gratis and for nothing!…

JULIE: Am I not the prize for it?

DE LA BRIVE: Méricourt wouldn't be capable of putting me…

JULIE: Ah! you don't love me!

DE LA BRIVE: *(Aside)* Oh! I just fell for a plot device from a novel. *(Aloud)* Even if your father owed millions, I would still marry you, for I love you! Ah, you're a very skilled actress, and I won't go back on my word. You'll make a splendid ambassador's wife….

JUSTIN: *(Enters, to* JULIE*)* Mam'selle, Monsieur Pierquin wishes a word with your father *(Undertone )* concerning Monsieur de la Brive, I believe.

JULIE: My father is in there. *(She points to the inner rooms.)*

PIERQUIN: *(Enters)* Mam'selle, I'm at your service.

DE LA BRIVE: *(Aside)* Pierquin here! *(He turns his back on him and examines the pictures through his lorgnette.)*

PIERQUIN: *(Aside)* Why, it's my Michonnin! All is lost! And me learning he's marrying an heiress, I come here to retrieve his I O Us… That devil of a Mercadet's a lucky dog, he knew how to lure him into his clutches!..

JULIE: Do you know this gentleman?

PIERQUIN: You're a sly one! I see you're in on the plot and you're guarding him! *(Aside)* Oh! I wish I had a pretty niece to do things like that!

JULIE: Who is he?

PIERQUIN: Michonnin! A debtor who's never around. Don't let go of him, I'm going to alert the fraud squad!

JULIE: To arrest Monsieur de la Brive?

PIERQUIN: We know him as Michonnon!

JULIE: The gentleman isn't rich?

PIERQUIN: Fodder for debtor's prison, he put his personal property in a friend's name.

JULIE: Ha! *(She laughs.)*

PIERQUIN: *(Aside)* Mercadet has robbed me. *(To* JULIE*)* Keep him amused and your father will be able to pay me the forty-seven thousand francs. After he's locked up, this young fellow-me-lad will be bailed out by some lovely lady.

JULIE: *(Aside)* Married and locked up, that's too much of the same thing!

JUSTIN: *(Enter, to* PIERQUIN*)* The master is occupied, as you know, with Mam'selle's marriage. He asks you to excuse him…

PIERQUIN: Marriage to who?

JUSTIN: Why, to that gentleman there! *(He points to* DE LA BRIVE *and exits.)*

PIERQUIN: Oh! *(Aside)* Two bankrupts getting married. The Stock Exchange will split it sides! …I'm on my way. *(He exits.)*

JULIE: Is your name Michonnin, sir?

DE LA BRIVE: Yes, Mam'selle, that's our family name. But, like so many others, for the last ten years we've called ourselves de la Brive by putting an M in front. It's more elegant. La Brive is a charming little estate purchased by my grandfather…

JULIE: Was that man telling the truth when he said you're in debt?

DE LA BRIVE: Oh, not much, minor nuisances. I told your father about it.

JULIE: So, sir, you're marrying me for love! *(Aside)* Let's have a laugh. *(Aloud)* And my dowry…

DE LA BRIVE: Mam'selle, you'll find me to be the most loving, the most loveable of husbands. A socialist, concerned with the most important matters of politics and my ambition, I will leave you in control of…your fortune…

JULIE: Sir, I have no fortune either…

*(*MERCADET *appears.)*

MERCADET: Daughter, so this is the consequence of your passion for that Minard boy, it prompts you to defame your father, to…

JULIE: To enlighten Monsieur Michonnin who, drowning in debts, cannot marry a girl with no money…

MERCADET: The gentleman's name is Michonnin?

DE LA BRIVE: Michonnin de la Brive…

MERCADET: Leave us, daughter.

JULIE: *(Undertone to her father)* Pierquin just left to have this gentleman arrested, I hope you won't allow it. What role would I have played?

MERCADET: *(Looks at his watch)* The sun's gone down! Too late for arrests. Has Pierquin seen the gentleman?

JULIE: Yes!

MERCADET: The devil's taken a hand in my game.

*(*JULIE *exits.)*

DE LA BRIVE: *(Aside)* The wedding's off!.. I'm no longer a socialist. I'll be a communist.

MERCADET: *(Aside)* Hoodwinked as if I were at the Stock Exchange! by Méricourt, my wife's friend! It's enough to stop believing in God!..

DE LA BRIVE: *(Aside)* Let's live up to our name!..

MERCADET: *(Aside)* There's an ease in how he did it. Shall we take the high ground? *(Aloud)* Monsieur Michonnin, your conduct is worse than despicable!

DE LA BRIVE: How so, sir? Didn't I say I was in debt?

MERCADET: All right. Anyone can be in debt. But where is your estate located?

DE LA BRIVE: In Les Landes.

MERCADET: It consists of…

DE LA BRIVE: Sand, planted with fir trees…

MERCADET: Good for making toothpicks?

DE LA BRIVE: That's about it.

MERCADET: And it's worth?

DE LA BRIVE: Thirty thousand francs.

MERCADET: Mortgaged for?

DE LA BRIVE: Forty-five thousand!

MERCADET: Well, that shows some talent!

DE LA BRIVE: Indeed it does!

MERCADET: Hell, that's not so dumb! And your marshes?

DE LA BRIVE: On the coast-line.

MERCADET: So, right smack in the ocean!

DE LA BRIVE: The people in those parts were malicious enough to say so and so my borrowing's been cut short!

MERCADET: It would be very difficult to borrow money on the ocean.

DE LA BRIVE: It'd have to suffer a sea change.

MERCADET: A deep-sea change. Sir, between you and me, your morality seems to be ...

DE LA BRIVE: That'll do!

MERCADET: Iffy!...

DE LA BRIVE: Sir, if it's only between you and me...

MERCADET: According to a note I've seen on certain acceptances, all your personal propety is in a friend's name, you sign your I O Us Michonnin and call yourself De la Brive.

DE LA BRIVE: Well, sir, what about it?

MERCADET: What about it? ...I could do you a very nasty turn.

DE LA BRIVE: Sir, don't go too far. I am your guest...

MERCADET: And by means of these subterfuges you want to worm your way into a respectable family, abuse the confidence of a father and mother... you pretend to love my daughter! *(Aside)* This fellow can be put to use. He's got looks, he's elegant, clever... *(Aloud)*... you are a ...

DE LA BRIVE: Don't say it, it could cost you your life...

MERCADET: My life! You are my guest, sir...

DE LA BRIVE: Once and for all, sir, does your daughter have a dowry or not?

MERCADET: Sir?

DE LA BRIVE: *(Aside)* I'm his equal and in a stronger position. *(Aloud)* Sir, do you have two hundred thousand francs?

MERCADET: My daughter's virtues...

DE LA BRIVE: No, you do not have two hundred thousand francs... And I was pawning my precious freedom! Am I not a valuable property? You were trying to entrap a son-in-law!

MERCADET: That word's a bit harsh.

DE LA BRIVE: You deserve it.

MERCADET: *(Aside)* He keeps his cool!...

DE LA BRIVE: Now I see it, you were taking advantage of my inexperience. I could lodge a complaint as well.

MERCADET: The inexperience of a man who can raise a loan on sand sixty percent above its value.

DE LA BRIVE: You can make crystal out of sand.

MERCADET: Now there's an idea!

DE LA BRIVE: So you see, sir, our morals have much in common!

(MERCADET *flinches.)*

DE LA BRIVE: Ah! between you and me...

MERCADET: *(Aside)* I'm going to squash him flat!... *(Aloud)* You're wrong there, sir, you are my debtor and I've got you dead to rights. Pierquin handed me forty-eight thousand francs' worth of your I O Us with interest and costs. I can have you locked up for five years.

DE LA BRIVE: Then, sir, I will be your guest!

MERCADET: Don't take that tone with me! Are you scoffing at your debts, your signature?

DE LA BRIVE: Aren't you?

MERCADET: *(Aside)* That's my business! *(Aloud)* Just what is your situation?

DE LA BRIVE: Desperate… Méricourt is marrying me off because I owe him thirty thousand francs above the value of my furniture.

MERCADET: I get it. I won't amuse myself by reading you a sermon, you would prefer a thousand franc banknote…

DE LA BRIVE: Oh, be my father-in-law!

MERCADET: No, our two wretched plights add up to one massive heap of destitution, but listen to me!

*(Enter* MME MERCADET.*)*

MME MERCADET: Will this gentleman be staying for dinner?

MERCADET: Of course. In difficult circumstances, dinner aids reflection. *(Aside)* I have to get him drunk to find out the inner man.

DE LA BRIVE: My despair gives me an appetite!…

MERCADET: Let's have dinner!

MME MERCADET: I can hear Verdelin's carriage!

MERCADET: What am I going to say to Verdelin?

JUSTIN: *(Enters in formal livery)* Monsieur Verdelin.

*(*JUSTIN *exits as* VERDELIN *enters.)*

VERDELIN: *(To* MERCADET*)* I didn't bring Madame Verdelin and I don't even know if I should dine with you.

MERCADET: *(Aside)* He's furious. *(Aloud)* The lady's hand.

*(*VERDELIN *kisses it grudgingly.)*

MERCADET: Now leave us.

*(*MME MERCADET *and* DE LA BRIVE *exit.)*

MERCADET: Well, what's come over you?

VERDELIN: Was that your son-in-law?

MERCADET: Yes and no.

VERDELIN: Is that the fine match!

MERCADET: *(Aside)* He knows everything! *(Aloud)* The marriage, my dear Verdelin, is not going to take place, Méricourt tricked me! Méricourt! You know what he is to us? But…

VERDELIN: But me no buts. This morning you played me one of your comedies with your wife and daughter in the cast to get your hands on a thousand crowns! I thought as much. That was neither subtle nor…

MERCADET: Don't go on, Verdelin! That's the way men in difficulties are judged… They're suspected of the very worst! …Why would I have borrowed your dinner service? Would I have dressed up my wife and daughter without a hope of this marriage? …In the first place, who told you that Julie's marriage was called off?

VERDELIN: I ran into Pierquin…

MERCADET: So people know about it?

VERDELIN: Everyone's laughing at you! You're got a briefcase full of your son-in-law's I O Us. Pierquin told me that your creditors are getting together tonight at Goulard's to act tomorrow in unison.

MERCADET: Tonight! Tomorrow! I hear the tolling of the bankruptcy bell!…

VERDELIN: They want to rid the Stock Exchange of fraudsters, as much as possible.

MERCADET: Imbeciles! …So tomorrow they're going to bring me down?

VERDELIN: To debtor's prison, in a closed carriage!

MERCADET: The speculator's hearse! Let's go to dinner!

VERDELIN: The dinner will cost me too much, I'd never digest it! No thanks!

MERCADET: Tomorrow the Stock Exchange will recognize Mercadet as one of its leaders! Come to dinner, Verdelin, don't worry. *(Aside)* Let's go! *(Aloud)* All my debts will be paid! …And the house of Mercadet will be dealing in millions!.. .I shall be the Napoleon of high finance.

VERDELIN: What a man!

MERCADET: And without a Waterloo.

VERDELIN: And your troops?…

MERCADET: Cash…cash on demand! What can anyone say to a businessman who declares, "The cash-drawer is open!"

VERDELIN: I'll dine with you after all, and I'm delighted. Long live Mercadet, emperor of speculators!

MERCADET: They asked for it! Tomorrow I will either lord it over millions or sleep in the clammy shroud of the Seine!

END OF ACT THREE

# ACT FOUR

MERCADET: *(Rings)* Let's find out what effect my measures have had.

JUSTIN: *(Enters)* Sir?

MERCADET: Justin, I should like the arrival of Monsieur Godeau to be kept secret…

JUSTIN: Oh, sir, that cat's out of the bag…Monsieur Brédif has already gone to spread the news…the racket the travelling carriage made driving into the courtyard at two o'clock this morning woke up the whole house, and Monsieur Brédif first of all! He thought the master was running away to Brussels…

MERCADET: Oh really! He's going to get paid…

JUSTIN: The master can't be serious!

MERCADET: You suppose you're my secretary already! I forgive you, Justin, for you know how I think!

JUSTIN: That carriage is spattered all over with mud, sir, but old Grumeau noticed that it wasn't carrying any baggage…

MERCADET: Godeau was in such a hurry to get here and right his wrongs towards me that he left his luggage at Le Havre. He's back from Calcutta with a rich cargo, but his wife stayed behind. Yes, he finally married his son's mother for she was devoted enough to go out there with him.

JUSTIN: It's awfully lucky the master was up all night working, for he was able…

MERCADET: To meet Godeau at the door! In your place! You'd been carousing! And got tipsy, Monsieur Justin!

JUSTIN: We only drank the heel-taps!

MERCADET: If you could spread it around that there is no Godeau, it would dampen the zeal of my creditors, and I could treat with them for more moderate terms…

JUSTIN: *(Aside)* The sly fox! If this man doesn't get rich, it'll be a hell of an injustice!

MERCADET: Send old Grumeau to my unlicensed broker….

JUSTIN: Monsieur Berchut! Rue des Filles-Saint-Thomas… Is old Grumeau allowed to tell him about the arrival of Monsieur Godeau?

MERCADET: Justin, you'll make your fortune. Go on! Be sure no one disturbs me until I ring for you.

*(Exit* JUSTIN.*)*

MERCADET: *(Alone)* When Mohammed had three colleagues he could trust (the hardest kind to find), he had the world in his grasp! I've already got Justin. The second? …Let's not go overboard! If people believe that Godeau is back, I gain a week, and when it comes to payment, one week means two! In Godeau's name I'll buy three hundred thousand francs' worth of Basse-Indre stock this morning, right away, before Verdelin has the chance. And then, when Verdelin, who thinks I'm out of the running as a competitor and who never intended to include me in this deal, puts in his order, my broker will send it sky-high! …What's more, last night, I wrote a letter in the name of several shareholders to demand publication of the report Verdelin's agent is suppressing… My broker will have this letter printed in all the newspapers. In no time at all, stocks will rise twenty-five percent above par. I'll make a six hundred thousand franc profit. With three hundred thousand I'll pay for the purchase. With the three hundred thousand left over, I'll pay off my creditors. Freed from debt, I'll be king of the mountain! *(He struts about majestically.)* I've been busy! …Went in person and ordered a four-wheeled travelling carriage from a garage in the Champs-Élysées, as if I intended to make a midnight flit! I kept an eye out for that damned driver who almost spoiled everything by thanking me at the top of his lungs… The tip was too big! My mistake! Now, it's between the two of us! *(He opens the door to his bedroom.)* Michonnin! the police are here!

(DE LA BRIVE *enters in a panic.)*

MERCADET: Calm down! …It's a wake-up call!

DE LA BRIVE: Sir, a drinking bout is to my brain what a summer storm is to the countryside, it refreshes, it makes things grow! And ideas sprout and flourish! … *In vino varietas!*

MERCADET: Yesterday, my dear friend, we were unfortunately interrupted in our business dealings…

DE LA BRIVE: Father-in-law, I remember perfectly well. We realized that neither of our firms could any longer meet its obligations. We are going… (as they say in the financial world) to be executed. You have the misfortune to be my creditor, and I have the good luck to be your debtor to the tune of forty-seven thousand, two hundred and three-francs and seventy-nine centimes.

MERCADET: Despite the hangover, your head's not heavy!

DE LA BRIVE: Neither is my purse or my conscience! How can anyone reproach me? By devouring my fortune I made money for every trade in Paris, even the ones nobody knows about! We, useless? …We, idle? Not a bit of it! We love to keep money in circulation…

MERCADET: With the money already in circulation!

DE LA BRIVE: Yes, when I've spent it all, I pay a high price for more, isn't that a way to honor it? People have made it into a god, I never begrudged dropping coins in the plate!

MERCADET: Oh, you've got your intelligence about you!

DE LA BRIVE: That's all I' ve got!

MERCADET: But that is our mint for coining money. Well, given your current mood, I will be brief…

DE LA BRIVE: Then I'll sit down, papa! Because you look deucedly as if, as we gentlemen riders say, you've got the bit between your teeth.

MERCADET: In business, one has the right to be ingenious…

(DE LA BRIVE *makes a gesture.)*

MERCADET: Sir, extreme ingenuity is not impropriety, impropriety is not laxity, laxity is not dishonesty, but put them all together and they fold into each other like a telescope.

DE LA BRIVE: *(Aside)* He didn't get me drunk for my benefit!

MERCADET: Eventually the nuances become imperceptible, and so long as you don't overstep the law, if you're blessed with success…

DE LA BRIVE: Ah, right you are, success…I said it once and the saying caught on… Success is often a bitch goddess!…

MERCADET: Two minds with but a single thought!

DE LA BRIVE: Sir, many intelligent people share common ground with us.

MERCADET: I see you on a slippery slope which leads to that audacious ingenuity for which fools condemn shrewd operators! ...You have tasted the tart, intoxicating fruits of Parisian pleasure. Vanity has sunk its steely claws deep into your heart! You have made luxury the inseparable companion of your existence! For you, Paris begins at the Place de l'Étoile and ends at the Jockey Club! Paris, for you, is the company of women who are talked about too much or not at all...

DE LA BRIVE: Indeed.

MERCADET: It's the heady atmosphere of wits, newspapers, the stage and the corridors of power, a vast sea to fish in! Either you carry on with that existence or you blow your brains out...

DE LA BRIVE: No! To carry on with it without any...

MERCADET: Do you feel you have the genius to keep yourself in patent leather boots, to live up to your vices? To dominate minds by the power of capital, the force of your intelligence? Will you always have the talent to tack between those two promontories on which elegance founders: the cheap hashhouse and the debtor's prison?

DE LA BRIVE: You break into my conscience like a burglar, you echo my thoughts! What do you want of me?

MERCADET: I want to save you by launching you into the world of business.

DE LA BRIVE: How?

MERCADET: Be the man to compromise himself for me...

DE LA BRIVE: Men of straw may be burnt.

MERCADET: Be inflammable.

DE LA BRIVE: Do you have insurance?

MERCADET: Give it a try! Serve me in the desperate plight I'm in and I'll give you back…your forty-seven thousand, two hundred and thirty-three francs, seventy-nine centimes… Between you and me, all you really need is nerve…

DE LA BRIVE: Pistol, sword…

MERCADET: No one will be killed. On the contrary…

DE LA BRIVE: That suits me.

MERCADET: We have to bring a man back to life.

DE LA BRIVE: That doesn't suit me at all! My dear friend, the last-minute legacy, the miser's cashbox, buried treasure, all the plot devices that made us laugh in antiquated plays get the cold shoulder in real life. These days police inspectors interfere and you can't beat them with a stick, not since the abolition of feudal privileges.

MERCADET: How about five years in debtor's prison, eh? Do you prefer that sort of sentence!

DE LA BRIVE: True enough! It all depends on what you want a man to do! …Because my honor is intact and worth the trouble to…

MERCADET: You want to invest it well, but we have too great a need of it not to draw on it for all it's worth! You see, so long as I'm still on my feet, I have the right to found companies, float projects. They've killed off our premium. Investments are dying from a dividend anemia, but our ingenuity will always be more potent than the law! They'll never kill off speculation. I've understood my era! Today, any deal that promises an immediate gain beyond its face value…whatever it is, even if it's a mirage, can be doable! You're selling the future, the way the lottery used to sell the dream of its impossible odds. So help me to stay seated at the Stock Exchange's well-laid table and we'll feed one another to the point of indigestion!...for you see, those who chase after millions may have a hard time finding them, but those who don't never find them!

DE LA BRIVE: *(Aside)* A person might go in with the gentleman!

MERCADET: Well?

DE LA BRIVE: You'll give me back my forty-seven thousand?

MERCADET: Aye, aye, sir!

DE LA BRIVE: I only have to be very devious!

MERCADET: Ooh, ooh! Say, careless! But this carelessness will be, as the English say, on the right side of the law!

DE LA BRIVE: What do I have to be?

MERCADET: Something like an uncle from America, my partner from India.

DE LA BRIVE: Is that all!

MERCADET: You will buy depressed shares so you can sell them when they rise.

DE LA BRIVE: By word of mouth?

MERCADET: I have my company signature! My partner, for we are still partners, used it to endorse the funds he stole from me in 1830. I have the right to use it against him today...

DE LA BRIVE: It's risky, damn it!

MERCADET: Only if someone spots you, recognizes you...

DE LA BRIVE: I'll give up the role as soon as I've turned over to you forty-seven thousand, two hundred and thirty-three francs and seventy-nine centimes.

MERCADET: A noise? Justin is eavesdropping! *(Loudly)* Come in, Godeau, you'll be the ruin of me! Go and lie down!…

*(He pushes him into the bedroom.)*

JUSTIN: *(Through the door)* Sir, it's your broker Monsieur Berchut.

MERCADET: *(Opens the door)* Good morning, Berchut. The Basse-Indre stocks, did they fall yesterday?

BERCHUT: Like a stone! Monsieur Verdelin sold some at twenty-five percent below the subscription price. The panic will be over this morning like it never happened!

MERCADET: If the stock market's price should fall fifteen percent beyond yesterday, I'll take two thousand shares.

BERCHUT: *(Pulls out his notebook and calculates)* That'll be three hundred thousand francs.

MERCADET: That's what I figured! At par, they'll be worth six hundred thousand.

BERCHUT: What date for payment and what collateral will you give me?

MERCADET: Collateral! …For shame! It's a done deal. Bring me the shares, I'll pay for them!

BERCHUT: Given your situation, you're obviously buying on Godeau's behalf.

MERCADET: Godeau!

BERCHUT: I know he's back…

MERCADET: Hush! if people hear about it, I'm lost… Who told you?

BERCHUT: My clerk wormed it out of your concierge.

MERCADET: Ah, I forgot to shut his mouth with a gold piece.

BERCHUT: You should send Godeau's carriage to a garage. If your creditors (for I understand you plan to go into liquidation), if they see it, they'll be unyielding…

MERCADET: Oh, to get hard cash they'll make a few small sacrifices. Fresh money, after all!…

BERCHUT: Yes, it pays off!… *(Aside)* There's always something to gain with his devil of a fellow… Let's keep on his good side! *(Aloud)* All right, Monsieur Mercadet, if it's for Godeau!

MERCADET: *(Aside)* Well, well! And away we go!

BERCHUT: Have him give me a written order and that'll be enough!

MERCADET: *(Aside)* Saved! *(Aloud)* He's asleep, but as soon as he's up, you'll have the order..

BERCHUT: It's a deal then. Goulard and two other operators paid me a commission to sell at all costs.

MERCADET: To be paid…

BERCHUT: In ten days.

MERCADET: Send the shares to Duval, for Godeau, my dear fellow, did me the disservice of taking him as his banker.

BERCHUT: *(Aside)* And he was right to do so!

MERCADET: It's petty, but what can I say? He's overflowing with good intentions towards me! Not a word! We're going to go into business together again. From now to the end of the year I foresee a hundred thousand francs' worth of commissions from us.

BERCHUT: Can I buy Basse-Indre on my own account?

MERCADET: *(Aside)* Another colleague I can trust… *(Aloud)* Yes, but talk it down to the inside traders! Here!… *(He hands him a letter.)* …Insert this letter in all the papers, and make an announcement when you've bought the shares.... Between you and me, when the Stock Exchange opens, they'll have gone up fifteen percent! Keep the secret of Godeau's return, deny it!... *(Aside)* He's going to blare it all over town.

*(*BERCHUT *exits as* MME MERCADET *enters.)*

MERCADET: *(Aside)* Fine! Here comes my wife! In cases like these, women spoil everything, they get nervous!... *(Aloud)* What do you want, Madame Mercadet? You've got a face like a funeral.

MME MERCADET: Sir, you were counting on Julie's marriage to re-establish your credit and placate your creditors, but yesterday's events have put you at their mercy.

MERCADET: That's what you know about it!

MME MERCADET: Can I be of any use?

MERCADET: *(Aside)* I'm going to get her out of the way by treating her rudely. *(Aloud)* Use! You! For the last eighteen months you've been going out with Méricourt and you have no idea what he's like: he's got money, he's Michonnin's creditor! You'll never be anything but a good housewife! You want to be of use? ...Look, the weather is splendid! Order a barouche, get dressed, you and your daughter... and have lunch at Saint-Cloud in the Bois de Boulogne. You 'd be doing me a great favor...

MME MERCADET: *(Aside)* He's hatching something against his creditors, I want to know what it is.

*(*MERCADET*, to his daughter who is crossing the stage:)*

MERCADET: Are you going to keep flitting through the apartment like that? I want to be alone to face my creditors...

*(*JULIE *returns immediately, followed by* MINARD.*)*

JULIE: Father, it's...Adolphe...

MERCADET: Fine! Sir, do you still want my daughter?

JULIE: Yes, Papa.

MINARD: Yes, sir. I made my desire known to Monsieur Duval, who has been a father to me since I was nine. And as he was there when Mam'selle Julie was born, he strongly approved my choice. He said, "She's like her mother, a treasure of honor, with solid qualities and no ambition..." Mam'selle Julie has forgiven me for my fear that she has no money...

MERCADET: You were right. I don't want Julie to marry a man with no fortune...

MINARD: But, sir, unbeknownst to me, I had a small fortune all along...

MERCADET: Bah!..

MINARD: When my mother entrusted me to Monsieur Duval, she handed him a sum of money which good old Duval invested instead of using it for my upbringing. This little capital has now grown to thirty thousand francs... Learning of your problems, I begged Monsieur Duval to turn this sum over to me, and I bring it to you, sir. Sometimes if you pay a bit on account an arrangement can be made...

MME MERCADET: *(Wiping away tears)* What a good young man!

JULIE: *(She squeezes* MINARD*'s hand)* Very good, very good, Adolphe!

MERCADET: Thirty thousand francs! *(Aside)* It might be tripled if I bought some of Verdelin's gas stock and that would be a way to.. No, no! *(To* MINARD*)* My boy, you are still young enough to make grand gestures. If thirty thousand francs were enough to pay off two hundred thousand, the fortunes of France, myself and the whole world would be a sure thing… No, keep your money!

MINARD: You refuse it?

(MME MERCADET *embraces him.)*

MERCADET: *(Aside)* I shall make them wait patiently for a month. I might, with a few audacious moves, bring extinct shares back to life; but the money of these poor children, it would break my heart… Never make plans when sobbing. The only money one should gamble with is that of investors… No, no! *(Aloud)* Adolphe, you shall marry my daughter.

MINARD: Ah, sir! Julie, my Julie!

MERCADET: As soon as she has a dowry of three hundred thousand francs…

MINARD: Ah! Sir, how long are you making us wait?

MERCADET: *(Aside)* I'll sell the two thousand shares only at twenty-five percent above par… *(Aloud)* In a month's time. And you can do me a favor…

(MINARD *holds out his wallet.)*

MERCADET: Put away your wallet, it's making me itchy! …Take away my wife and daughter. *(Aside)* What a temptation! but I resisted. If, at last, I do succumb, I'll grow their little capital, I'll manage their funds for them… My little girl is loved… What hearts of gold! Dear children, I shall make them rich… Let's go and rehearse my Godeau. *(He exits.)*

MINARD: I would so like to right my wrong!

MME MERCADET: Ah! Monsieur Adolphe, at least misfortune serves to identify those who are really in love…

JULIE: I won't thank you, for I have all my life for that! But, Adolphe, the moment when I was proud, proudest of you will lie like a diamond in my heart shining whenever we celebrate at home.

MME MERCADET: My dear children! ...If your father were willing to pay off his creditors, if he could retire from business and live in the country, what more would we need to be happy? ...Oh! how I sigh for a honest, calm obscurity! How tired I am of this specious opulence, this shunting between luxury and poverty, the jostling of speculation!

JULIE: Don't worry, mama, we shall triumph in the Stock Market!

MME MERCADET: What it would take to convince your father would be the kind of disasters I wouldn't wish on him! ...Ah, here comes the hardest-hearted of his creditors, always shouting and threatening...

(GOULARD *enters.)*

GOULARD: Madam, forgive me for disturbing you, I don't want to intrude, I've come to see if I can help out my dear friend Mercadet...

MINARD: *(To* MME MERCADET*)* Why, he's most polite.

JULIE: *(To her mother)* Father must have come up with some ploy...

MME MERCADET: *(Aside)* He scares me. *(To* GOULARD*)* He'll be here soon.

GOULARD: I've learned of the happy event that changes the state of your affairs.

JULIE: Monsieur Goulard, tell us the truth, we're in the dark!

GOULARD: *(Aside)* She's a slyboots!

MME MERCADET: Sir, for heaven's sake, what event?

GOULARD: The return of his partner, Godeau.

MME MERCADET: Sir! Daughter! Adolphe! Ah! What joy! …Sir, you have seen Godeau! Has he come back a rich man?

GOULARD: You know very well, he disembarked at your house… you gave a dinner for him, but he came too late…

MME MERCADET: Godeau, here! …Last night?

GOULARD: I saw his travelling carriage.

JULIE: Yes, mama, a carriage did come last night…

MME MERCADET: Sir, I swear no one came to my house last night…

GOULARD: Very well! Madam, you're marvelously in tune with Monsieur Mercadet's interests! He taught you to recite this lesson,

MME MERCADET: Sir…

GOULARD: But he won't be able to hide Godeau from us for long! …We'll wait…a month, if necessary. Besides it's known on the market floor, where all his creditors got together this morning. Godeau has already bought two thousand shares of Basse-Indre… A weak start! You can see he's just back from India, he's not up-to-date on investments!

MME MERCADET: Sir, you're talking Greek…

GOULARD: All right, I'll talk turkey. Look, madam, I'll make a slight discount in what's owed me, if you find a way for me to meet with Godeau…

JULIE: Sir, my mother and I understand nothing about business!

GOULARD: *(Aside)* This rascal knows how to exploit his wife! And that air of artlessness the mother and daughter can put on! I must get a wife!…

MME MERCADET: *(To* GOULARD*)* Sir, I shall send you my husband. *(To her daughter)* I'm worried your father's gone too far... If he wants to send us away, it's because he's afraid of what we might do. Oh! this time I shall keep an eye on the goings-on.

*(*JULIE *and* MME MERCADET *exit.)*

GOULARD: Listen, sir, I know you're marrying Mam'selle Mercadet, Duval told me. If old Duval consented to this marriage, it's because he knows of Godeau's return, because Godeau trusts no one but Duval. Your broker knows all about it!

MINARD: This is the first I've heard of Monsieur Godeau's return.

GOULARD: Perfect! You consider yourself a member of the family, so you're in on this conspiracy of silence! ...Now look here! this is in Mercadet's interest. Tell Godeau that, if he's willing to pay me on the spot, I'll make a discount of twenty percent.

MINARD: Sir, I haven't the least right to meddle in Monsieur Mercadet's affairs, not yet, and I think he would take it amiss if I... Anyway, here he is...

MERCADET: *(Enters)* My dear Adolphe, the ladies are waiting for you. *(Undertone)* Take them to lunch in the country or you'll never have Julie.

MINARD: I promise. *(He exits.)*

MERCADET: So, Goulard! Yesterday I was told you've all decided to force me into bankruptcy? You claim I'm a swindler...

GOULARD: You! One of the most able men in Paris! A man who'll make multimillions...as soon as he has the first one.

MERCADET: So you all gathered together to...

GOULARD: To figure out how to help you! We'll wait, dear friend, for as long as it takes.

MERCADET: A day late and a franc short! Still, you have my thanks, my dear fellow, just as if you'd made that remark yesterday morning…

*(Enter* JUSTIN.*)*

MERCADET: What do you want, Justin?

JUSTIN: *(Undertone)* Sir…Monsieur Violette is offering me sixty francs if I let him in to see Monsieur Godeau…

MERCADET: Sixty francs! *(Aside)* The ones he wheedled out of me!

JUSTIN: The master wouldn't want me to miss out on a good deal?

MERCADET: Let him corrupt you! You're becoming very much a secretary and I leave him to you… fleece him…

JUSTIN: Oh! down to the skin!

MERCADET: Goulard! If I may? …I have to pen a short note in reply to what Justin just told me… *(He exits.)*

GOULARD: I get it…

JUSTIN: Monsieur is so shrewd!

GOULARD: How much did Violette out there offer you to get in to see Godeau?

JUSTIN: The gentleman knows that Monsieur Godeau…? No, he didn't offer me a thing.

GOULARD: What did he give you?

JUSTIN: To betray my master who gave me strict orders to conceal the arrival! …Well, ten louis!

GOULARD: Here's fifteen, my lad!

JUSTIN: *(Aside)* Ah! if only Monsieur Godeau could return more often!

GOULARD: So I'll be the first to see him! Debts owing to the amount of seventy-five thousand francs.

JUSTIN: If the gentleman will wait with Monsieur Violette in a side room, I'll alert you as soon as Monsieur Godeau has had lunch, for the master wants him to be served in this drawing-room.

GOULARD: All right! *(He exits.)*

JUSTIN: I'll put them all in there, one by one, like fish in an aquarium.

*(*MERCADET *enters.)*

MERCADET: Well!

JUSTIN: I'm waiting for the master's orders for when I can let them see Monsieur Godeau.

MERCADET: Go on, my boy, make hay while the sun shines, and don't dare eavesdrop on what Godeau and I are saying. *(Aside)* He's going to glue his ear to the door!

*(*JUSTIN *exits.)*

MERCADET: *(Once he's alone)* It's scary how like Godeau he looks, at least the way I imagine he does after ten years in India… Come in…

DE LA BRIVE: *(Disguised as a nabob)* Ah, my dear friend, what a dreadful climate, this Parisian climate! If my son didn't live here, I would never have returned, but, it was high time the poor boy found out his father and mother got married….

MERCADET: *(Makes a noise at the door and rings)* Honestly! You must have been on the stage? The makeup is superb…

DE LA BRIVE: My first conquest in 1827 was a duchess of a certain age who loved to play romantic leads. She had a theatre on her estate in Touraine.

(JUSTIN *enters.)*

MERCADET: A light! for the gentleman's hookah. You will serve the gentleman's tea here on this table.

JUSTIN: Sir, Pierquin is trying to bribe the concierge!

MERCADET: Let him in as soon as my wife and daughter have gone out. *(He lights the bowl of the hookah.)*

JUSTIN: He's treating him like the first investor in a new stock company… *(He serves lunch.)*

MERCADET: Let's write a note to Duval asking him to back me up. He's very puritanical. Bah! since he's fond of Julie, he'll save me. *(He writes downstage. To* JUSTIN*)* Have the concierge take this note to Duval.

(JUSTIN *exits.)*

MERCADET: It's an awful risk! But if Basse-Indre stocks stay below par?

DE LA BRIVE: What'll happen to you then?

MERCADET: Bah! Luck of the draw, fifty percent pro, fifty percent con.

(GOULARD *and* VIOLETTE *enter.)*

GOULARD: *(To* VIOLETTE*)* Didn't I tell you! He's guarding him like reserve capital.

VIOLETTE: My dear Monsieur Mercadet…

MERCADET: Excuse me! I'm busy…

GOULARD: We know who with…

MERCADET: I doubt it…

VIOLETTE: The good Monsieur Godeau!

MERCADET: What fairy tale are you spinning! …I declare, Violette old man, this gentleman is not Godeau. As Goulard is my witness!

GOULARD: *(To* VIOLETTE*)* He's lying like a corporate prospectus, but all's fair in business.

VIOLETTE: Otherwise commerce would be in a bad way…

GOULARD: Anyway, although the gentleman is in native dress, I recognize him… Come, come, Mercadet, don't try to deny it.

MERCADET: I don't deny that Godeau… *(He raises his voice)* Godeau, who cheated me out of all I had, I would like to be able to say to all of Paris that honest, discreet, virtuous Godeau, a capable and energetic fellow, is on the way and just about to land.

VIOLETTE: We know him, he's back from Calcutta.

GOULARD: With a fortune…

MERCADET: An incalcuttable fortune!

GOULARD: Nice one! …He looks like a nabob.

VIOLETTE: How do you talk to a nabob?

*(*MERCADET*, to* VIOLETTE *who is stepping forward:)*

MERCADET: Oh! don't speak to him… How can you expect me to let him be…pestered by my creditors!

GOULARD: *(Who has slipped next to* DE LA BRIVE*)* Your excellency!

MERCADET: Goulard, if I may! …I won't allow it.

VIOLETTE: He's gone completely Indian.

MERCADET: He has changed a lot! India has that effect on people! You understand! Cholera, curry, chili peppers…

GOULARD: *(Next to* DE LA BRIVE*)* Pay me what your friend Mercadet owes me and I'll discount twenty percent.

DE LA BRIVE: Do you have the bills?

MERCADET: Oh, Goulard!

GOULARD: My friend, he's only asking to pay!

*(*MME MERCADET *enters. When she opens the door we can see a group of creditors.)*

MERCADET: *(Aside)* Great! She's going to do something stupidly honest that will be the death of me…

MME MERCADET: *(To the two creditors)* Gentlemen, stop! Monsieur Mercadet is the victim of a bad joke *(Looking at* DE LA BRIVE*)*, I would like to believe, which must not harm your interests…

GOULARD: Madam!

MME MERCADET: This gentleman is not Monsieur Godeau.

MERCADET: Madam!

MME MERCADET: *(To* MERCADET *with fire and authority)* You have been duped, sir, by a schemer…

VIOLETTE: How so, madam?

MME MERCADET: Gentlemen, if you keep quiet about this escapade which I do not wish to give a worse name, you will be paid.

GOULARD: And by whom, if you please, my fair lady?

MME MERCADET: By Monsieur Duval!…

*(The two creditors flinch and consult one another.)*

MERCADET: She's going to…going to…

MME MERCADET: Go and see him this evening, you'll find me there, and all of Monsieur Mercadet's creditors will be satisfied.

VIOLETTE: Oh! in that case!…

*(Exit* VIOLETTE *and* GOULARD.*)*

DE LA BRIVE: Madam, if you weren't a woman…I am Monsieur de la Brive.

MME MERCADET: You, Monsieur de la Brive? No, sir, you're not!

MERCADET: What gall! This isn't like her…

DE LA BRIVE: What? am I not me?

MME MERCADET: Monsieur de la Brive is a young man whom I was able to observe yesterday at dinner. He knows that debts are no disgrace for anyone who owns up to them and works to pay them off. He is honorable, he will pay them, for he has his whole life ahead of him and too much intelligence to want it blighted forever by a scheme punishable by law…

DE LA BRIVE: Madam, I really and truly am…

MME MERCADET: I don't want to know who you are, sir! But whoever you are, I think you should appreciate the favor I am going to do by stopping you on the brink of an abyss…

DE LA BRIVE: Madam, your husband inveigled me into it by promising to give back the promissory notes that stand between me and my future…

MME MERCADET: Sir, my husband is an honest man and he will make you a gift of them!.. We will be satisfied with your word and you can pay them off when you have made your fortune honestly.

DE LA BRIVE: Ah, madam, you have opened my eyes! I am Monsieur de la Brive once more. I must tell you that from this moment on I shall fearlessly travel the road of hard work.

MME MERCADET: The right road, sir, that of honor, is difficult, but Heaven will bless all your efforts!

MERCADET: *(Aside)* That's one way to gain credit! Rely on it, young man!

DE LA BRIVE: How can I thank you enough? I shall be a son to you the rest of my days.

(DE LA BRIVE *kisses her hand respectfully, bows to* MERCADET *and goes into* MERCADET*'s bedroom.)*

MERCADET: Ah! alone at last! You've just ruined me, madam! My liquidation will take place as if by magic! You must have access to, I won't say El Dorado, but the printing press of the Bank of France.

MME MERCADET: No, sir, I have access to honor.

MERCADET: Aha! Is it next door to a fortune?

MME MERCADET: Oh, no jokes, sir. I am a poor woman without any special knowledge but that of the heart. The intuition that informs us about the interests of the man whose name we bear told me you were about to gamble a fortune against dishonor. Forgive me, I would bet more on dishonor than on the fortune. I want you to remain honest, upright, courageous, everything you've been up to now.

MERCADET: Up to now I was standing firm, but you've just knocked me as low as the Haitian loan.

MME MERCADET: Sir, these may be what you would call a woman's fancies, but do me the favor to listen! I may still have two hundred thousand francs, take them to pay off all your creditors.

MERCADET: And then what? We'll be as poor as Spain!

MME MERCADET: We'll be rich in reputation.

MERCADET: What next?

MME MERCADET: Your daughter and son-in-law, your wife and you, sir, well! we'll go to work! …Yes, we'll start life over with Adolphe's little capital and we'll earn the fortune needed to live in an average decent life. There are a thousand ways to make a fortune. But I know only one good one that the solid middle-class should never have abandoned: making money by hard work and honesty, not by scheming… Patience, wisdom, thrift are three homely virtues which preserve all they give. Don't hesitate, sir. You have a wife who loves and respects you, children who cherish you! … Let's leave this atmosphere of lies and deceit, this specious opulence which doesn't fool anyone any more. If all we have is a crust of bread, we'll eat it in good spirits, and it won't stick in our throats like the delicacies at those feasts where fortunes are gulped down and people laugh at ruined investors…

MERCADET: *(Aside)* Once admit your wife is right and you're forever a zero in your own home. Women claim to be forgiving, but their forgiveness comes and goes, like fits of ague.

MME MERCADET: You hesitate!

MERCADET: You have just undone, with the best of intentions, the fortune I had finally found… and you want me to thank you. You're beginning to judge me?

MME MERCADET: No, sir, I do not judge. *(Aside)* Ah, I've got an idea! *(Aloud)* Let me consult two upright, pure hearts, whose delicacy has not yet been tainted by contact with the world. Be so kind as to step into your study for two minutes…

MERCADET: Really?… *(Aside)* I'll use the time to consider what to do next.

MME MERCADET: Children, come in…

*(*JULIE *and* MINARD *enter.)*

MINARD: Here we are… What do you want?

MME MERCADET: Your father is in an even worse plight than I thought and, as he puts it, it's a matter of win or die. Now, with a great deal of deception and audacity, he could pay his debts and gain some time to make a fortune. Our assistance and our wits are needed to make so bold a plan succeed. What if everyone believes in Godeau's return, what if you, Adolphe, were to disguise yourself and impersonate him?…

(MINARD *winces.)*

MME MERCADET: Monsieur Mercadet could buy shares in his name and get heavy discounts from his creditors… The shares would rise and pay off everything in a short time: purchase price and creditors… We would need the cooperation of Monsieur Duval…

JULIE: Oh, mama! Your affection for my father is making you delusional! Forgive me! He can't have devised such a plot and I wouldn't marry Adolphe if he…

MINARD: Oh Julie!… *(He kisses her hand.)* Madam, ask for my life and all I possess! But to take part in such a… Oh! I'll go and implore Monsieur Duval to lend his support to Monsieur Mercadet. But think, madam, what you're asking? …It's a…

MME MERCADET: *(Quickly)* Swindle!

MINARD: It's much worse! Suppose it were a complete success, a man would still be dishonored! …It's a cr…

JULIE: Adolphe! Don't say it!

MINARD: In the name of all you hold most dear, madam, give up such an idea! Bankruptcy is a better way. People recover from it, and here…

MERCADET: *(Enters)* Adolphe! You would marry a bankrupt's daughter?

MINARD: Yes, sir! For I would work to rehabilitate him!…

(MERCADET, *his wife and daughter surround* MINARD.)

MERCADET: *(Aside)* I give in!… *(To his wife.)* You are a good and noble creature! *(Aside)* How many men would seek such a treasure! Once one has her, it's madness not to sacrifice everything for her… *(Aloud)* You deserve a better fate!

MME MERCADET: Ah, sir! this is what you were like before Godeau absconded.

MERCADET: Yes, for I am ruined but honest! Oh! I'm lost!… *(Aside, in such a way as to be heard.)* I know what I have to do! *(He exits.)*

MME MERCADET: I tremble! Children, don't leave your father alone!

*(They all run after* MERCADET.*)*

END OF ACT FOUR

# ACT FIVE

*(*JUSTIN *is the first to enter and makes a sign to* THÉRÈSE *to come in.* VIRGINIE*, laden with her account books, plumps down on the sofa. He looks through the keyhole and glues his ear to the door.)*

THÉRÈSE: They've got a nerve hiding their affairs from us.

VIRGINIE: Old Grumeau says that the master is going to be arrested. I want repayment for what I laid out. That's what's due me, that money, not to mention my wages owing!

THÉRÈSE: Take it easy, we're going to lose everything. Ever heard of a bankruptcy?

JUSTIN: I can't hear a thing, they're talking too low. The master still doesn't trust us.

VIRGINIE: Monsieur Justin, just what is a bankruptcy?

JUSTIN: It's a kind of court-approved thievery, but spoiled by obligations. Keep calm, word is the master will liquidate instead.

VIRGINIE: What in the world is that?

JUSTIN: Liquidation is the same as bankruptcy, but complicated by a declaration of the debtor's good faith…which eliminates the obligations.

THÉRÈSE: What a know-it-all, that Justin!

JUSTIN: Those are the master's words, I'm his disciple!

BRÉDIF: *(Enters unseen)* This time I'll have my apartment back not in three months but in two weeks! There's been lots of expensive improvements. He had the drawing-rooms gilded. Oh, I'll get a thousand crowns more in rent…

*(The servants all go far upstage to be unobtrusive.)*

MERCADET: *(Done in)* What do you want, Monsieur Brédif? Your apartment? You shall have it!

BRÉDIF: *(Aside)* I'd like to see him gone, but this devil of a fellow has resources. *(Aloud)* Sir, you will find it very natural that I should be much more interested in a tenant than in people like creditors who wear out the steps on my staircase.

MERCADET: Oh! that I should inspire pity!..

BRÉDIF: You know I own the house next door to this one, rue des Ménars. Listen: at the bottom of the garden, there's an exit door opening into the courtyard of that other house.

MERCADET: So what?

BRÉDIF: If you want to make an escape…

MERCADET: What for?

BRÉDIF: Everyone knows your situation…there's talk of issuing a writ…

MERCADET: Oh! behold all the horrors of insolvency, the slow death of a businessman's honor!… *(He sees the servants.)* What are you doing there? Go away!

JUSTIN: We'd love to, sir, but we're waiting…

MERCADET: What for?

THÉRÈSE: Our wages…

MERCADET: Go to Madame Mercadet, she'll pay you.

*(The servants run out.* MERCADET *to* BRÉDIF:*)*

MERCADET: My dear Monsieur Brédif, I am staying put.

BRÉDIF: You don't realize the dangers threatening your position?

MERCADET: My position…is excellent.

BRÉDIF: He's out of his mind…

MERCADET: What would you give me to break my lease? You would gain three thousand francs a year, seven years makes twenty-one thousand francs. Let's come to terms!

BRÉDIF: *(Aside)* No, he's not out of his mind. *(Aloud)* But, my dear sir…

MERCADET: My fortune is about to be pillaged, I must do what bankrupts do: save my bacon.

BRÉDIF: Don't you know that if a complaint is lodged I must be a witness?

MERCADET: Witness to what?

BRÉDIF: That the travelling carriage arrived empty!

MERCADET: You're driving me crazy! Ah, my wife was right. Brédif, go to the cab stand in the Champs Élysées,..

BRÉDIF: What for!…

MERCADET: You'll see more than one empty carriage! You'll see hundreds of carriages… all of them empty…

BRÉDIF: *(Aside)* Oh, his creditors won't have an easy time of it. *(Aloud)* Your servant, Mercadet.

MERCADET: With all my heart!

*(Exit* BRÉDIF.*)*

MERCADET: *(Alone)* How greedy! …It's the way of the world! The river swallows up the stream…

*(Enter* BERCHUT.*)*

MERCADET: *(Aside)* Berchut! Ah! here's my punishment! Come, let's wallow in the swamp of humiliation. Brédif passed the sentence, Berchut is the first shot fired! *(Aloud)* Good morning, my dear Berchut.

BERCHUT: Good morning, my dear Monsieur Mercadet!

MERCADET: Your face reads twenty degrees below. Didn't the Basse-Indre stock go up?

BERCHUT: Indeed it did, sir. Word on the street has it we'll reach par this morning; then at the Stock Exchange, nobody knows how high it'll go! It's on fire. Your letter worked wonders. The company caught wind of the deal, it made public on the Exchange the result of its diggings, and the Basse-Indre mine is now worth as much as Belgian coal…

MERCADET: You followed my advice? How much did you buy for yourself?

BERCHUT: Five hundred!

MERCADET: *(Puts his arm around his waist)* That's thanks to me! But I'm delighted that you've pocketed …ha, ha! maybe a hundred thousand francs. Madame Berchut wanted a carriage, she shall have it! …My dear fellow, pretty women having to go on foot make me grieve… but when it reaches twenty percent above par, sell out!

BERCHUT: *(Aside)* He's a king among men, he's never hurt anyone but his investors.

MERCADET: And here's another piece of advice: give up insider trading! Remember that great line from the Gospels applicable to business matters: he who lives by the sword will perish by the sword!

BERCHUT: You're a fine one to talk! Look, between ourselves, you're facing implacable enemies. *(He pulls out a document.)* People are saying that this order is a forgery!

MERCADET: A forgery! ...It's in my handwriting...

BERCHUT: So Godeau isn't in Paris!

MERCADET: What, you too! Go to Duval, there you'll find the money owed you for the two thousand shares... What have you to say to that, old friend?

BERCHUT: Once Monsieur Duval pays me, I'll leave this paper with him. But, my dear Monsieur Mercadet, I hope for your sake Godeau turns up...

MERCADET: You are a worthy man, Berchut. *(Aside)* I just stepped into an even nastier mess!..

BERCHUT: *(Aside)* 'Pon my word, anyone but me would have strung him up. *(Aloud)* I'm off to Duval's. *(He exits.)*

MERCADET: *(Alone)* Well, well! ...I'm ruined, I'll have to send Adolphe to Duval. *(He shouts into the other room.)* Adolphe! Adolphe!

*(*MINARD *enters.)*

MERCADET: My friend, run to Duval's. Get him to pay off Berchut and I'm saved!

MINARD: I fly to your aid. *(He exits on the run.)*

*(*MERCADET *notices* VERDELIN, PIERQUIN *and* GOULARD *talking with* VIOLETTE *and his other creditors)*

MERCADET: Ah! the enemy is advancing.... I should have worn armor...I wish I'd gone for a stroll in leafy suburban groves.

*(*JUSTIN *enters.)*

MERCADET: Goodbye, Justin, you are losing a good master.

JUSTIN: *(Aside)* I'm not yet strong enough to leave my master. *(Aloud)* I'll stay by the master for another ten days.

MERCADET: Has my wife settled with you lot?

JUSTIN: Virginie is so hard-headed!.. with her, one and one always make three, before you've explained to her that one and one make…

MERCADET: One …

JUSTIN: *(Aside)* The master's always good for a laugh! Trouble brings out the wit in him!

*(*JUSTIN *withdraws.* VERDELIN, GOULARD, PIERQUIN *and* VIOLETTE *enter.)*

VIOLETTE: Ah, my good sir!

MERCADET: Well, well, good old Violette! What do you want? It's all falling apart, even a frame of iron! Bah! I'm not the only one, the membership is enormous.

VIOLETTE: No, no and no! Men such as you are rare! You should have sons… Paying off the interest, the costs! …Money down, cash on the barrelhead. I made a nuisance of myself, I beg your pardon, I'd stopped believing Godeau would return.

MERCADET: Say again? …The joke's a stale one.

GOULARD: My dear friend, I misread you, I'm devoted to you… This is sublime.

MERCADET: Ah! they've come for their revenge!

PIERQUIN: I haven't the gift of gab, not me! Just one word: Perfection!

VERDELIN: It's a joy to be your friend! We're proud to know you!

PIERQUIN: What a pleasure to do business with you!

VIOLETTE: I'd like to leave you my money.

GOULARD: You are the most honorable of men, for we would all have offered discounts…

PIERQUIN: Honorable! He's an ancient Roman out of Plutarch!

VERDELIN: And so accommodating!

MERCADET: Oh really! Gentlemen, are you done ridiculing my misfortune?.. You laugh! But I've come to an awesome decision, and I'm delighted to have you all here. I speak the truth, if you don't grant me time to pay, I'll cut my throat, here, in front of you! *(He pulls out a razor.)*

VERDELIN: Put away that argument, my dear fellow. Everyone has been paid by Godeau.

MERCADET: Godeau! …But Godeau is a myth! Godeau is a fairy tale! Godeau is a phantom…you know it as well as I do.

ALL: He's back…

MERCADET: From Calcutta?

ALL: Yes!

GOULARD: With an incalcuttable fortune, as you said.

MERCADET: Oh really! you taunt a bankrupt this way!

BERCHUT: *(Runs in)* Sorry, extremely sorry! My dear Mercadet, here are your shares: they've been paid for.

MERCADET: Who by?

BERCHUT: By Godeau, just as you said.

MERCADET: *(Takes him aside)* Berchut, you wouldn't, you that I enabled to make….

BERCHUT: A hundred and fifty thousand! We're at par.

MERCADET: You saw Godeau…

BERCHUT: He told me these shares were for you.

MERCADET: Godeau!

BERCHUT: In person! …Landed at Le Havre.

BRÉDIF: *(Enters)* Mercadet, here are your receipts… *(Aside)* I won't get my apartment back.

MERCADET: I'm dreaming!

*(*MINARD *enters.)*

MERCADET: Adolphe, you'll tell me the truth! Godeau…

MINARD: My father is in Paris, sir, and, as you said, a year ago he married my mother. Now that I'm acknowledged his legitimate heir, my name is Adolphe Godeau.

MERCADET: He paid these gentlemen?

MINARD: Everyone, scrupulously. He also paid Berchut and begs you to keep those shares as your portion in the profits of his ventures in India…

MERCADET: Hail, Chance, Queen of Kings, Archduchess of loans, Princess of stocks and bonds and mother of credit! Hail, Fortune so sought after here but who, for the thousandth time, comes from the Indies! …Oh, I always said Godeau has such an active heart…. And such honesty! …But go and call in the ladies!

*(*MERCADET *pushes* MINARD *into the other room.)*

MERCADET: Gentlemen, I am charmed to….

BERCHUT: I dare hope you'll continue your trust in me.

MERCADET: My dear fellow, I am saying goodbye to speculation.

VERDELIN: We shall withdraw and leave you with your family. As to the thousand crowns, I give them to Julie to buy two diamond studs.

MERCADET: Now that he's recognized his debt, I can't recognize him.

*(The creditors exit.* MME MERCADET, JULIE *and* MINARD *enter.)*

JULIE: Papa, what a beautiful soul! Adolphe is a millionaire and he's still marrying me...I don't know if I...

MERCADET: Don't get on your high horse!

MME MERCADET: Oh, my dear!... *(She weeps.)*,

MERCADET: But you were so courageous in adversity...

MME MERCADET: I have no strength at the joy of seeing you safe... and rich....

MERCADET: Rich but honest... Look here, wife, children, I must confess... Well, I was at the end of my rope, so worn out I was going under...my mind constantly on edge, always a chip on my shoulder! ...A giant would have succumbed... There were times I wanted to run away... Oh! to able to rest!

MINARD: Sir, my father just bought an estate in Touraine, be his neighbor. Do as he does, spend part of your fortune on land!...

MME MERCADET: Oh, my dear, the countryside...

MERCADET: Whatever you want!

MME MERCADET: You'll get bored.

MERCADET: No, after all those dirty deals, I'll deal in dirt! Agriculture will be my occupation! I'd like to study it as a money-making proposition... Let's go!

*(*MERCADET *rings.* JUSTIN *enters.)*

JUSTIN: The master rang?

MERCADET: Call a carriage... *(Aside)* I've put Godeau to use so many times I've got the right to see him. *(Aloud)* Let's not keep Godeau waiting!

*(Curtain)*

END OF PLAY

www.ingramcontent.com/pod-product-compliance
Ingram Content Group UK Ltd.
Pitfield, Milton Keynes, MK11 3LW, UK
UKHW020134250726
13967UKWH00002B/647